WHEN PEOPLE SPEAK FOR GOD

by

Henry E. Neufeld

Energion Publications
P. O. Box 841
Gonzalez, FL 32560
http://www.energionpubs.com
pubs@energion.com

Energion Publications
P. O. Box 841
Gonzalez, FL 32560

Cover Design and illustrations by Jason Neufeld, jasonneufelddesign.com.

ISBN: 1-893729-38-9

ABOUT THIS BOOK

This book began as a compilation of previously written material. I have written several essays that I published on the web, both on my Energion.com Webzine and on my blogs. Biblical inspiration, the gift of prophecy, God speaking to people, and people claiming that God told them certain things very often will become part of the discussions when I'm teaching in person. A number of readers of the internet material have suggested I get it in print, as they find reading 50-60 pages at a time on screen difficult. Those who attend my classes often ask me for something they can read for more information on what I teach about inspiration. Thus far I've referred them to URLs, often an unsatisfactory option.

My original plan was to collect the essays, write a couple of connecting or explanatory notes, add topical and scripture indexes, and publish. Ah, that was wishful thinking! I may be the boss but I'm an incredibly *cruel* and *evil* boss. Thus when I looked at the collected essays I said to myself, "This won't do at all. Get thee to work!" (Note that the archaic language is not an indication of divine inspiration.)

The backbone of the book is my essay *Inspiration, Biblical Authority, and Inerrancy*, which you can check out on the web at http://rpp.energion.com/inspired.shtml. It has been edited and scattered throughout the book where it logically fits in. The illustrations have also been redone by Jason Neufeld (jasonneufelddesign.com). Added to this is material on the modern gift of prophecy, and practical considerations for handling the situation when someone claims divine authority for their words. You'll find almost all the remaining material in this book by checking out the *Biblical Inspiration* category on both my *Threads from Henry's Web* blog (http://www.energionpubs.com/wordpress) and my *Participatory Bible Study Blog* (http://www.deepbiblestudy.net).

Besides the print format, this book provides you with better organization, a **Table of Contents**, a complete **Scripture Index**, and a fairly detailed **Topical Index**.

I would like to acknowledge a number of teachers who saw me through my own struggles with Biblical inspiration.

- ✔ My uncle Pastor Don F. Neufeld who got me started studying Greek

- ✔ Prof. J. Paul Grove, at Walla Walla College who worked with me through the servant passages of Isaiah

- ✔ Dr. Alden Thompson at Walla Walla College who saw me through Biblical Hebrew and Old Testament history

- ✔ Dr. Malcolm Maxwell, Walla Walla College, who challenged my theology and exegesis at all times

- ✔ Prof. Lucille Knapp, Walla Walla College, who taught me to see the human side while also teaching me Greek grammar

- ✔ Dr. Leona Glidden Running, Andrews University, my graduate advisor who taught me about the importance of empowering women in the church while also teaching me Middle Egyptian and Akkadian

- ✔ Dr. Larry Geraty, Andrews University, who encouraged me to think about publishing. It took around 25 years, but I eventually headed that way!

- ✔ Laney Beard, who read parts of this book and made suggestions that helped me to clarify it.

- ✔ My wife Jody, who listened to numerous selections, helped me with wording, and who is also patient enough to live with someone who is obsessively editing a manuscript!

All errors, weaknesses, and heresies are, of course, totally my own. I do not in any way intend to suggest that these wonderful people would necessarily endorse my conclusions.

I hope and pray that this collection helps you in your own efforts to hear God speak to you.

PREFACE

This book is the result of practical experience and personal exposure to the Bible. It is not going to summarize all the theological positions that the church has ever held on the inspiration of scripture. It's not going to be a work of deep theology. I also intended it to be short, about 80-100 pages in 12 point font, but as I write this I'm threatening 200 pages, and it may get a bit larger than that. (It ended up around 275 pages.) Nonetheless I'm going to try to keep it straightforward and practical.

The question people ask me when they come for prayer or advice is this: How can I know what God's will is for my life? Now I could respond by telling them that the Bible is completely inspired in every word, known as *verbal plenary inspiration*. But what exactly does that mean to you? I could respond by stating that the Bible is historically and scientifically inerrant, but nobody has ever come to me for prayer over a historical or scientific issue.

What people want to know is precisely what God expects of them. The want to know God's will and purpose for their lives. They think they can find that out in the Bible, but they aren't sure how. Often they have tried reading, but they haven't managed to get the answers that they are looking for.

It seems to me that the answers we give in theology classes and in churches tend to miss the point. I also think many of those answers are wrong, but that's actually a less important issue. If one has the means of pursuing the answer, then it is much less important whether one has arrived at an answer yet. With the means, answers will come.

I see a similar problem with Bible study and prayer. Often when we try to make a case for the power of prayer, we emphasize that God answers prayer. There's the acronym PUSH—pray until something happens. We conduct scientific studies on whether or not prayer works. But we miss the simple fact that prayer is not a means to make God do the things that we want him to do. If prayer was the means by which we could trigger desired responses from God, then such scientific tests might be relevant. But prayer is about us having a conversation with God. Prayer is successful if you have that conversation. Only you know whether that is taking place, and you are the only one who needs to know.

Bible study is similar. You will find out soon enough that I don't accept the doctrine of Biblical inerrancy. That scares some people, because they believe that the Bible is their standard, and the idea that their standard for living might contain errors is frightening. But that ignores a great deal of what the Bible itself is about. Again, it's a matter of conversation.

I believe that most of us come to the Bible looking for *information*, while God comes to the Bible looking for *conversation*. These are not mutually exclusive options. But if our focus is not similar to God's, either in prayer or in scripture reading, then I think we will tend tomiss the point.

In fact, over time I have come to see less and less difference between my devotional times that are spent in prayer and those spent in Bible study. I can speak to God during either time, and I can listen for God to speak during either time.

Some years ago I worked for Radio Shack. One function of a salesman is to match the customer to just the right item or part. An elderly lady, clearly not too comfortable with technology, came in to buy a "telephone cord." Now at the time, "telephone cord" could mean any of a number of things. One type of cord would connect the handset to the base unit. A few different types of cords could connect the telephone to the wall jack as well. It took a few minutes for me to get it clear that the cord she wanted connected the phone base unit to the wall jack. I was hoping both ends would be RJ-11 or 14 plugs, but just to make sure I said, "What does the other end look like? Let me show you the possibilities."

"It doesn't have any other end," she replied.

Now I want you to know that I did figure out the correct "other end" for her cord, and she went home a satisfied customer. But I think that many people view prayer and Bible study as a sort of one-ended cord. Doctrines of inspiration tend to be essentially doctrines of God. God is perfect, so the Bible must be perfect. So what? I have to read it, interpret it, and apply it, and I'm a very imperfect person.

In order to have an effective understanding of inspiration, we have to understand both ends of the cord, and in this case the cord is much more like a network, with extenders along the way, and we have to understand how each of those connections work as well.

In this book I plan to examine the function of inspiration by looking at how it happened, and how it happens. Most books about inspiration are solely about scripture—the written text. We write separately about the gift of prophecy in the church today and the words of scripture. Some people have become quite angry when I try to combine them, as though it was unfair.

One person with whom I discussed this issue on the Internet was offended by this question: When you hear a voice, how do you know it's the voice of God? He said, "We're not talking about hearing voices. We're talking about the Bible!"

But when God tells Abraham to leave his country and go to a place he didn't know, he was hearing a voice. He may have been having a vision. We don't know. But whether it was an ordinary voice, or a voice in a vision, he heard a voice. But he didn't have any written scripture. Because he followed the voice that he heard, we have scripture. There are many, many people in the Bible who heard voices. If you are disturbed by people hearing voices, you probably should choose something other than the Bible as your reading material.

Think of one end of this telephone cord as God, and the other as human beings. On the one hand, many conservative Christians see the one and only critical element to be the sovereignty and power of God. In the Calvinist tradition, God chooses who will be saved and then saves them. We talk about human activity, but there is no point in the process at which Calvinism allows human activity to be significant. The cord has just one end! It may be people who are saved, but the people don't have a function in that process other than to be acted upon.

On the other hand, many liberal Christians put the focus so thoroughly on humanity that the only thing that matters is what a human being can do and become. God is again effectively outside of the loop. The cord has one end—it's just the opposite end.

Now please don't remind me that many Christians, Calvinists, conservatives, liberals, and others, are not at the extremes I've described. I know that. That's why they are called *extremes*. But I do know that the extremes exist, and I believe there are many who might not like the description who nonetheless behave as though the cord has only one end.

So my goal here is to look at how people hear from God, how their writings might be accepted and collected (by them or others), how those might come to be a part of scripture, and then how we can hear God's voice through that scripture. But it's also about how someone living today can hear God's voice, then relate what they heard by

x

speaking or writing, while listeners respond. What is the appropriate way to go about testing, understanding, and applying this?

Think about this: If you heard a voice, one you thought was audible and not just in your head, and it told you to pack all your earthly goods and put them in a moving van and move, but told you that you would be told your destination after you drove the moving van out of the driveway, how would you react?

If you're a Christian, and you said, "No way," you may need to think a bit about your use of the Bible. That is precisely what Abraham did. Jesus followed what his Father told him, and walked right into crucifixion. Are you comfortable in their company?

If you're not a Christian, this book will be of less interest to you. I'm not trying to prove the inspiration of the Bible or of prophets from outside the community, testing them by some objective standard. I am looking at how they are used in Christianity and how they can function. I don't totally ignore objective tests here, but they are not my main focus.

Let's explore these ideas together.

But as if, in all the instances of this covering (i.e., of this history), the logical connection and order of the law had been preserved, we would not certainly believe, when thus possessing the meaning of Scripture in a continuous series, that anything else was contained in it save what was indicated on the surface; so for that reason divine wisdom took care that certain stumbling-blocks, or interruptions, to the historical meaning should take place, by the introduction into the midst (of the narrative) of certain impossibilities and incongruities; that in this way the very interruption of the narrative might, as by the interposition of a bolt, present an obstacle to the reader, whereby he might refuse to acknowledge the way which conducts to the ordinary meaning; and being thus excluded and debarred from it, we might be recalled to the beginning of another way, in order that, by entering upon a narrow path, and passing to a loftier and more sublime road, he might lay open the immense breadth of divine wisdom.

-- Origen, De Principiis, Book IV.15

TABLE OF CONTENTS

GOD AND MAN

What is the main reason we are concerned about the Bible and its inspiration?

Generally, the answer to that question is simple. We want to know about God and his will for us. How much we're willing to get involved with God is another question. For many of us, just having a guide to making good ethical decisions is sufficient. Others would like a detailed road map for all of life's decisions. In either case, Bible students are generally asking what God's will is in their life.

Often people don't look very much at that Bible they trust to find out just what it means to them.

It's very easy to discuss the Bible for years and even write about it, without answering this very basic question. Some people are satisfied with just the affirmation. "You can trust the Bible," says the pastor from the pulpit, and that's all they need. Almost as often, they don't really look very much at that Bible they trust to find out just what it says, how it says it, and how they are supposed to figure out what it means to them.

Let's think about inspiration in practical terms for a little bit. By "thinking in practical terms" I mean the way in which we use our understanding of inspiration when we apply what we learn from inspired writings.

We talk about inspiration in an extremely God-centered (source centered) way. Now being God-centered is not a bad thing, but in this case it can be misleading. I would suggest that while our theories of inspiration center around God and what he can and does do, our processes and principles of interpretation generally center around us as human beings and what *we* can do. This shouldn't be surprising, considering the amount of effort that must go into understanding any message, especially the message of scripture. It's also clear that interpretation is done by *people*, and thus they would be the focus when we talk about that activity..

If we do not get the right message, where is it that the information is lost?

The most important question is this: If we do not get the right message, where is it that the information is lost? Our wildly different interpretations of the Bible mean that somewhere some folks, likely very many, are not getting the right message. There are a number of places that the information could be lost. It could be that the prophet did not accurately hear the message. Perhaps a scribe copied it incorrectly, or a translator chose the wrong words. Finally, an interpreter might have simply misapplied God's words and produced something harmful or even very slightly in error.

No matter how accurately we believe God gave the message, in practical terms we are much more interested in how accurately we can understand it. Let's say that 2% of the message of the New Testament is lost by copyists. By that I mean that 2% of the text of the New Testament is not what the authors originally wrote. I think that number is fairly high, because that is closer to the percentage of the text that is in dispute, and not all text in dispute is likely to be wrong. But even if that is the case, I suspect that if we compare interpretations, we will see that a much higher percentage must be lost by somebody in the process of interpretation.

I think this difficulty extends to the great divide between types of revelation, even the big one between general and special revelation. We cannot be satisfied simply to ask what information each type of revelation can provide. We must also ask how accurately we can comprehend it.

Thus the question is not only the accuracy of the content, but rather in what is to be conveyed, and how well we are capable of understanding it. I would presume God would write his character quite perfectly in nature, and yet that may be the hardest message to interpret. Some people prefer the immediate revelation of modern prophets or of dreams and visions. I too believe that God is as capable of speaking today as ever, and as likely to do so, but in that case we have the additional burden of deciding on the authenticity of the message, and we still need to interpret what we hear, especially if it is a vision or dream. Even a verbal message must be verified as to accuracy and then applied correctly.

The last person, and the decisive person, to hear from God is you.

This is one of the reasons I believe that the doctrine of inerrancy , an evangelical standard today, is not only wrong, it is inadequate. It deals only with the source. It seems to be a way of guarding the barn door after the cattle have departed. Interpretation has gone in a thousand directions while some are arguing that the message was absolutely correct at the starting point. In addition, somehow it's OK for us to lose part of the source in the process of copying–something acknowledged when inerrancy is postulated solely of the conveniently missing autographs–and yet if one supposes that instead something got altered on the way from God to the prophet, all revelation must immediately become suspect.

Revelation is of value when I comprehend and apply it, and assertions of its validity apart from adding the line "and you can understand it" are pointless. I think that is part of the reason why there is wisdom literature in the Bible. It's God's message, but you have to think about it and comprehend it. Who you are, and how you have exercised your mind will make a difference in what you will understand. Revelation is not a replacement for reason, nor in appropriate areas is reason independent of revelation.

No matter whether you are listening to a new idea, a message someone claims to have received directly from God, or the interpretation of a passage of scripture, your individual mind, enlightened by the Holy Spirit, is the final filter to separate sense from nonsense. The last person, and the decisive person, to hear from God is you. Even the firmest believer in the detailed accuracy of the text of scripture will realize that many interpretations of that scripture are nonsense.

THE HUMAN FACTOR

The human mind is probably the most neglected part of God's creation.

Before we try to tie this together, let's look a bit more at the human factor. This is the other end of the telephone cord. Inspiration is not just about God. It is about how God communicates with human beings. Thus it is not just about God's perfection; it is also about humanity's imperfection. It is not just about God's infinite perspective; it is also about humanity's finite capacity to understand.

The human mind is probably the most neglected part of God's creation. It is a wonderful element, one that has provoked some of the most profound philosophical and scientific writing. No, I don't mean merely that people think with their minds and then write philosophy and science. I'm referring to writing about how the mind evolved, how it functions, what consciousness actually is, and why the mind malfunctions from time to time. Those are all interesting topics.

My topic, however, is how Christians can choose to honor God with their minds, and why they should. (In this book I'm addressing Christians because that's my own faith group, not to imply that other people cannot honor God with their minds.) Sometimes it seems that every element of our faith is used against the human mind instead of in cooperation with it.

1. Our saving faith is sometimes seen as a termination of our ethical decision making
2. Dependence on God is often seen as dependence on him solely in a supernatural sense, what God can do for you miraculously, but not in the natural sense, what God has made possible through the creation
3. The inspiration of the scriptures is seen as bypassing the people involved, whether, prophets, secretaries, redactors, copyists, or readers
4. The church offices, especially those of teacher and prophet, are seen as bypassing good thinking when people are expected to obey merely because of the office

It's by their fruit that you'll recognize them.

5. Laziness replaces the hard work of good thinking, as when we accept something just because we saw it in a book, and it was written by someone holy
6. An appearance of piety can replace wisdom. When someone announces–"God said it, I believe it, that settles it!"–without being certain that God says it, that bypasses the human mind.

Thus it is not merely in dealing with inspiration that the human factor, and particularly the factor of the human *mind* tends to get left out, it is also an issue throughout Christian theology and many things are interpreted so as to leave out the human factor.

Still, it would seem that simply from observation and logic we could discover that God wants us to use our minds. He provided them. They are necessary to our survival. Even if we didn't have scriptural statements to confirm this, it is pretty obvious from nature. But we do, in fact, have scriptural confirmation.

How long, simple-minded folks,
will you love being simple?
How long will scoffers delight in scoffing?
And fools hate knowledge? — Proverbs 1:22 (NRSV)

Now I could spend my time listing texts that back this up further, texts that talk about thinking, wisdom, using our minds, and our choice. They are a strong theme in scripture. But I'm going to assume you either know or can find the texts. I'd just like to call your attention to two texts. The first is from the words of Jesus.

God has not abrogated the law of cause and effect in his kingdom.

[15]Watch out for false prophets, who come to you dressed like sheep, but inside they are ravenous wolves. [16]It's by their fruit that you'll recognize them. [17]People don't gather grapes from thorns or figs from thistles, do they? [18]A good tree cannot produce bad fruit, nor can a bad tree produce good fruit. [19]That's why you will recognize them by their fruit. — Matthew 7:15-19 (HN)

This is a sentiment that Paul repeats in Galatians:

[7]Don't be deceived! God won't be mocked! Whatever a person plants is what he'll harvest! — Galatians 6:7 (HN)

These two texts make it clear that God has not abrogated the law of cause and effect in his kingdom. The law of cause and effect is one that is basic to human thinking. It's clear that God wants you to think about the consequences of your own actions, not to mention the words and actions of others. What people think, what they say, and what they do does have consequences.

So how can one honor God with one's mind? Primarily by using it! Let's look at these ways in which we tend to undermine our minds in serving God.

It's sometimes difficult to maintain the relationship of faith, grace and the requirement for human decision making. Paul noted the same problem. My point is certainly not original with me–it's Biblical! Paul uses most of Galatians 5 and the first several verses of Galatians 6 dealing with the possibility that some would take their salvation as permission to sin. Some would decide that grace meant they could do as they pleased and not suffer the consequences. He makes it clear that's not what grace is about.

The best antidote to this type of thinking is for us not to regard salvation merely as a ticket to heaven, but as spiritual healing. When we think of it like that, we might find the question rather silly. If the doctor provides you with a cure for your disease, and does not charge you (a true miracle, I know), you have received the free gift of healing. But if you go home and say, "I want the disease, I'm going to get it back," you may well be able to make yourself sick again. You can't then complain to the doctor that his free gift failed. You set his gift aside.

Grace opens the door, grace makes it all possible, but no number of gifts will make you rich if you throw them all away.

Christians sometimes depend on Jesus to save them from sin, while at the same time they indulge themselves in destructive behavior. I've done a transformation of the story of Susanna (Daniel 13, from the apocrypha).[1] What struck me as I read and worked on presenting that story is that the elders who falsely accuse Susanna do everything possible to lead themselves into sin and eventual destruction. They dwell on their temptation. They hide the fact that they are being

---

1 From http://www.jevlir.com/?p=20, Susanna: A Transformation, last accessed 4/2/07.

tempted. They get as close to sin as they can. When eventually they are caught, everything that follows is inevitable.[2]

Christians are often like that. "Why won't God free me from my addictions?" someone asks, at the same time sitting with the object of his addiction readily available. Grace opens the door, grace makes it all possible, but no number of gifts will make you rich if you throw them all away.

We also often see depending on God solely in the supernatural sense. What do I mean by this? Suppose I'm ill. Amongst some Christians if I take medicine I am no longer depending on God. They would say I should have faith and expect God to heal all my diseases. But God is also the creator of the natural world, and works with, not against his natural laws.

The goal is to get people to think for themselves, and to listen to God for themselves.

The problem is that Christians take actions that will bear one form of fruit while expecting God's supernatural intervention to produce the type of fruit they desire. You're going to reap what you sow! I am not denying miracles, or asking anyone not to pray for them. I pray for God's power and God's action myself. But I also know from scripture that God normally follows the simple law of planting and harvesting, or as Jesus said, of bearing fruit.

God's supernatural power is not there to provide you with a license to ignore God's laws, whether moral or natural laws written in the fabric of the universe.

In the same way the inspiration of the scriptures is seen as bypassing the people involved, whether, prophets, secretaries, or readers. It is so much easier to use "God said" for anything in the Bible, so we are often tempted to just say, "God said." But while there are portions of the Bible that are identified as the words of God, but there are also

---

2 Susanna is part of the additions to Daniel in the apocrypha, which is part of the Catholic canon, but is not accepted by most protestants.

large portions which are not. I have even heard Job's friends quoted as what "God said," and they are soundly condemned by God right in scripture. It takes more work to find out what God is doing when he acts in history or in our own lives than it is simply to find a phrase that says what we want it to, and then to quote it, but it also means that very often we are ignoring what God actually meant, while taking on the appearance of affirming his word.

Those who see miraculous gifts continuing in the church tend to see supernatural church offices, such as prophet or apostle in the same way. If an anointed church leader says it, then one no longer has to think. This attitude enables church leaders who have fallen into sin to continue both in their sin and in church leadership. Members who observed and thought would likely discover wrongdoing. The supernatural sources of knowledge and authority replace the natural ones completely, along with the

When we start ignoring the law of cause and effect, laziness replaces the hard work of good thinking.

God put prophets and teachers in the church for a purpose–to help bring his word to the people. I'm going to be brief about this, but it's very important! Please think about it! Now that we can all enter the sanctuary with confidence (Hebrews 10:19), we should have as our goal getting everyone to approach God for themselves. The goal is not to teach people to accept what we, as teachers, prophets, or leaders, say, but rather to get them to think for themselves, and to listen to God for themselves.

In the same way the scriptures do not exist to relieve you of the task of thinking and choosing. They are there to feed you, inform you and train you. You will have to exercise your mind if you are going to get an accurate understanding of God's will in your study of scripture.

For the individual, the goal is to approach God individually, and not to depend on the teacher, preacher, or even prophet. It may be harder, but it's the right goal. This does not mean that you operate apart from the community. There should be accountability, but the best accountability results from everyone using every gift that they have to acquire and apply wisdom and knowledge.

Ignoring God's natural laws and overemphasizing the supernatural continues to produce bad fruit. When we start ignoring the law of cause and effect, laziness replaces the hard work of good thinking, as when we accept something just because we saw it in a book, and it was written by someone holy.

When something is in print it gains a new measure of authority. Some people think that just because it's in a book it must be true. Many who know that one can't trust it just because it's in print, will trust it because it's in a book written by someone well known. But I have a secret (not really!) to tell you. There are plenty of Christian books in print that contain misinformation. I'm not talking about differences of opinion—I'm talking about things that people from many different perspectives could agree were just factually wrong. I find, for example, that a distressingly large number of "insights" brought from Greek or Hebrew in popular books are simply wrong, while many others are at least misleading because they don't have the proper context.

What God says and what people say God says may well be two very different things.

When you get information from a book, you need to check references, and then you need to assure yourself that the references themselves are reliable. There are some facts making the rounds in Christian books that have simply been quoted so many times that everyone "knows" they are right, but nobody knows precisely where those facts came from. You need to check back to a primary source— the person who actually observed and recorded the data in the first place—whenever possible.

You are responsible for planting seeds in your mind. **You** are the one who is going to bear the fruit. You need to honor God with your mind by looking up the information.

An appearance of piety can replace wisdom. When someone announces–"God said it, I believe it, that settles it!"–without being certain that God says it, that bypasses the human mind. I have frequently been asked how overemphasizing God's sovereign power can possibly be a problem. But the truth is always important, and the fact is that God works through the natural.

It's easy to dishonor God while sounding extremely pious. I cannot count the number of times I have heard someone say, "I'm just doing what the Bible says," or "That is just God's word!" when they are not, in fact, correctly quoting the material or are taking it badly out of context. What God says for a specific situation should settle it, but what God *says* and what people *say* God says may well be two very different things.

Always remember: You will harvest what you plant, and you are the one who chooses what to plant! The human factor is critical.

If God if perfect, why can't he just see to it that we understand perfectly?

THE DIVINE FACTOR

But what does it mean then that our communication is with God? Many people want to find the one solid thing on which they can hang their thoughts and dreams, something that allows them to be sure that they are right. Thus they are comforted by the idea of a perfect communication from a perfect God.

So if God if perfect, why can't he just see to it that we understand perfectly?

Well, he can. There is nothing preventing God from making certain that there is no doubt about his will. But a moment's thinking about your own life and looking around you at the lives of others should be sufficient to convince you that God has not done so.

Nonetheless there are plenty of people who still think God has communicated perfectly, and that we could get it all right if he would just do so. Generally people who think this belong to groups that continuously shrink and splinter, because every disagreement must involve someone who is too stubborn, too stupid, or too demonically controlled to realize their error.

Since the one under the power of demons is not going to admit he is wrong, the group will have to split according to who supports which of the contenders, and they will separate, bemoaning how the devil won again by blinding brother or sister so-and-so's eyes to the obvious truth.

God could also have created us with minds that were unable to incorrectly process data. He would have had to use a *The speed* somewhat different process, because human *of a* evolution is not a tidy thing, and it has not produced *connection* a tidy human mind. Our perceptions are easily *is limited by* deceived, and we can be massively disagreeable. *the slower of* We're not even always—or even most frequently— *the two* certain of precisely why we made a decision. A *terminals.* couple of times when I was younger I bought a car and then regretted it later. Nonetheless, at the time I thought I was carefully selecting the car and buying it for all the right reasons.

Now I examine more testing data and let my feelings be overcome by actual test results. But there are still many things in my life that are not decided that way.

God chose to make us the way we are, capable of both major feats of learning and major disasters of stupidity, sometimes committed by the same person. Thus until we reach that other plane, we will have disagreements on what God meant, and it is very likely that all of us are wrong on some things.

It's easy to forget, but if you work with communications between devices, you learn right from the start that the speed of a connection is limited by the slower of the two terminals. Now many people, even communications professionals, don't recall the days of slow serial connections. You had hand-shaking to determine what sort of error correction each side of a connection could handle, and then you carried out communications using the best possible set of options.

It is the same way with our communication with God. It's limited not by who he is but by who we are. Any speculations of what God might have done are pretty useless in the face of what he has done!

GOD SPEAKS

INSPIRATION IN ACTION

There are many theories about how God inspires people to write his message. In discussing inspiration, I'm going to start from within the Christian community and specifically with the Bible. This process allows us to examine the elements of inspiration based on material that at least one community regards as inspired.

This method is somewhat circular, but there is no generally accepted set of criteria by which one can determine what is and is not inspired. If there were such criteria, whatever document contained them would clearly be the most authoritative religious work, by which all others would have to be judged.

> *There is no generally accepted set of criteria by which one can determine what is and is not inspired.*

Because we must test something that claims to be from God by standards that claim to be from God, the process is somewhat circular, though we can anchor it to more objective standards at some point. It will be critical throughout our discussion to keep in mind one simple question: What is God trying to accomplish through inspiration?

It may seem that the answer is obvious—God wanted to give us information. But as we study claims of inspiration, from ancient scriptures to modern prophets proclaiming a current word from the Lord, I'd ask you to keep an open mind on this issue. We have no way to know just what God is trying to accomplish except through his revelation to us.

Typically, Christians have found proof texts in scriptures that make comments about inspiration. "All scripture is inspired (or God-breathed) . . ." (2 Timothy 3:16). "No prophecy of the scripture came by human will . . ." (2 Peter 1:21). These texts are not only used to prove the inspiration of scriptures, but they also provide the foundation for an understanding of how inspiration works.

This Son is the brightness of his glory and the exact representation of his real essence. — Hebrews 1:3

We will never completely escape this type of circularity, though I think there are better ways to deal with the issue. Claiming that the Bible is inspired because it says so makes a very small circle. The Bible consists of many separate documents that were combined into the canon of scripture. Does a claim of inspiration in 2 Timothy apply to Genesis? If so, why? Should we perhaps be making our claims based on the authority of the church councils that settled the question of the canon? We're going to look at these issues further in the following chapters.

I most commonly hear 2 Timothy 3:16 quoted in this connection. I ask someone what inspiration means. "All scripture is God-breathed," comes back the answer. "God-breathed" is supposed to be obvious, but somehow the passage doesn't enlighten us as to what God breathes, how he breathes it, and what this means for the text, other than that it is profitable (2 Timothy 3:17). Another answer, that prophets speak as they are carried along by the Holy Spirit (2 Peter 1:21), doesn't really answer the question either.

The process of inspiration is important not only in terms of how we understand God to behave in connection with people, but also in telling us what we would expect to result. For example, those who believe that God dictates the precise words that a prophet or other inspired writer puts on paper must in turn believe that those words, and not just the message they express, are important, and that they must always be the best words for the purpose.

On the other hand, someone who believes that people receive impressions from God and then express them in human words will place a greater emphasis on the human side of the equation. The message is important, and it may be illuminated by knowing the person who speaks along with his or her cultural background and spiritual experience.

As the author of Hebrews expressed it:

God's message came at different times and in different ways.

> *¹In old times God spoke to our ancestors through the prophets in many portions and in different ways. ²In these last days, however, he has spoken to us through a Son, one whom he has made heir of everything, and through whom also he created the universe. ³This Son is the brightness of his glory and the exact representation of his real essence. He sustains everything by his powerful word. He performed a cleansing from sins and sat down at the right hand of majesty in the {spiritual/heavenly} heights. — Hebrews 1:1-3 (HN)*

God's message came at different times and in different ways, a process that, according to the author of Hebrews, culminated in God's message coming through a *person*, Jesus. In Hebrews 4:12 he continues by calling the Word "alive and active" again referring to the Word of God as portrayed in Jesus. Those who place a heavy emphasis on the words, rather than the message, should give serious consideration to the view of revelation expressed in the book of Hebrews. According to this one scriptural author, whom most scholars leave unidentified, inspiration doesn't always work the same way.

I would suggest that instead of looking for statements about how inspiration works in the scriptures, we should look at the scriptures themselves. There are many clues as to how inspiration works in the stories and the records of those who were inspired. There is no good reason to assume that those who **experienced** inspiration would also feel it necessary to **define** it. In fact, when we look at the scriptures we see no real effort to provide us with a theory of inspiration. There were simply people who claimed that they had a message from God, and they expressed it with some force under their various circumstances.

When we look at the scriptures we see no real effort to provide us with a theory of inspiration.

If we look at the evidence of the text itself it doesn't seem that in many cases we have words dictated by God. There are passages that claim to be "words of God" and others that don't. Perhaps it would be best to respect that distinction.

Other than Moses bringing the tablets of the law from Mt. Sinai, we don't have material actually written by God. Moses himself has various scribes chronicle the activities of the Israelites as they travel through the wilderness (Genesis 17:14, for example). This would appear contradictory to the notion that Moses himself wrote the Pentateuch, or that it was delivered as a whole by God to Moses. What need of scribes to record the details if God had provided the words already?

Elsewhere in scripture we have communication given through dreams, visions, direct prophetic oracles, and research. The books of Samuel, Kings and Chronicles make reference to previously existing sources. Luke, in his gospel, makes a point of the research that he provided. John the Revelator seems to have concocted a special form of Greek, unless one assumes he simply made an exceptional number of errors in grammar, in writing the book of Revelation. I would suggest it is because he is so excited in the emotional state that results from receiving the vision, and that he struggles with words as he tries to describe what he has experienced. This again is far from verbal dictation.

We have prayers and stories that seem to express ungodly views such as Psalm 137:8-9 and parts of Judges 4-5. In Psalm 137 the Israelites wish that the children of the Babylonians be treated as they have been treated. This is a natural desire, but not exactly a forgiving one. In Judges 4 and 5 Jael receives the Canaanite king of Hazor as a guest and then murders him by stealth. Her actions are celebrated.

We have variations in similar stories that can be observed by comparing Samuel-Kings and Chronicles, or the four gospels in many cases. Clearly there is something more than verbal dictation going on here. In fact, there seem to be quite a number of "somethings" going on.

There is something more than verbal dictation going on.

If you accept the Bible as your sacred book, you will likely also have to come to the conclusion that God has spoken in times past in very many different portions and in very many different ways.

REVELATION IN THE NATURAL WORLD

The term general revelation is used to refer to the information that is available about God simply because he is the creator. Just as an architect, an engineer, or an artist will reflect some of himself in his work, so God is reflected in what he creates.

Commonly general revelation is seen to occur also through history, but I believe that in history and personal experience general revelation overlaps special revelation. In fact, what we call special revelation is simply a recording of an individual's experience with

God.[3] The two forms do not overlap completely. By observing that we live in a particular type of universe, I can make certain assumptions about God's character, but never in detail, and rarely very specifically.

Special revelation lets me know much more specifically how it is that God relates to me at my particular time and place. If God speaks to me directly, that is special revelation. If God gives me a sign, that is also special revelation. This can, of course be extended to groups, churches, and nations. (My particular way of phrasing this is guided by my desire to answer the question I asked in the preface: How can I know God's will for me? For a more nuanced definition, consult a theological dictionary.)

God expects us to be informed by all of the means of communication that he has provided.

I said earlier that we tend to separate a doctrine of the Bible from a more general doctrine of how God communicates. If we ignore the way in which God communicates through the natural world, we will have similar problems. God expects us to be informed by all of the means of communication that he has provided.

As an illustration I recall a seminar on spiritual gifts, especially those gifts that involved speaking God's word, whether speaking prophetically or teaching from scripture. At one point a class member asked how they could know a certain thing about another person in the congregation. The question was asked with the best of intentions—the questioner wanted to know the best way to be of service to that person. Could she ask the Lord for a word, or a sign, and expect to get that information? I asked her what would be wrong with simply asking the person. She was ignoring

---

3 Note that one's experience may be quite information intensive. The vision in the book of Revelation (the entire book is a vision) is a good example. But John the Revelator experiences God. His experience is in the form of a vision.

one part of God's creation—our ability to speak, hear, and understand, in favor of a supernatural solution.

But the revelation through prophets, the supernatural revelation, and even the revelation through the person of Jesus Christ is not the whole of God's revelation. Paul tells us: "For [God's] invisible attributes, his unending power and divinity, have been understood and seen since the creation of the world" (Romans 1:20). I would suggest that this is a neglected text. Just how much can one learn simply from the creation without the benefit of direct revelation? Paul seems to think this revelation is sufficient that there is no excuse for missing the essentials of this revelation. Thus apparently one can derive from God's created things sufficient information to come into favor with God and thus for salvation, and this is clear enough that one cannot be excused for failing to understand. I don't think we give enough weight to the implications of this passage in Romans.

One can derive from God's created things sufficient information to come into favor with God and thus for salvation.

In particular, some Christians would hold that Paul's "without excuse," is theoretical. While the information is there, we are so perverse that we cannot actually see it. Thus we are "without excuse" but we have the excuse that we are actually incapable of comprehending the information that makes us "without excuse." It kind of goes round and round. Certain interpretations of original sin lead to this conclusion, in which humanity is to be blamed for sinning, but is in no way capable of stopping.

The Wesleyan doctrine of prevenient grace intervenes at this point for Wesleyan-Arminians, with its presentation of a God who sees our condition and helplessness, and extends grace to us before we ask, indeed, before we are capable of asking. For Calvinists predestination intervenes. Those who are predestined to be saved are enlightened by God.

In the late 4th and early 5th centuries CE, two powerful theological minds were in conflict over this very issue. Augustine held the doctrine of original sin in its strongest form. According to Augustine, human beings are not capable of seeking God or choosing good. Pelagius believed that human beings could choose either way. Calvinism was built on the pelagian understanding. If people can only choose the right by the power of God's grace, then those who receive God's grace do so, and others do not.

Jacobus Arminius, in the 16th century also opposed Calvinism. His doctrines have been preserved through the Wesleyan tradition. Wesleyan-Arminians are often accused of semi-pelagianism, or even outright pelagianism.

According to Augustine, human beings are not capable of seeking God or choosing good. Pelagius believed that human beings could choose either way.

According to Arminians, prevenient grace given to everyone which gives them a choice, thus nobody is predestined. Doctrinally there is a difference, but the effect is that every person has a choice for good or for evil. The opportunity is provided by God, but the individual must nonetheless choose to accept it.[4]

But Paul continues later:

> [12] *All who have sinned apart from the law will also perish apart from the law, and all who have sinned under the law will be judged by the law.* [13] *For it is not the hearers of the law who are righteous in God's sight, but the doers of the law who will be justified.* [14] *When Gentiles, who do not possess the law, do instinctively what the law requires, these, though not*

---

4   I'm certain that practically all Wesleyan theologians would disagree with me here, believing that there is a more substantial difference between pelagianism and prevenient grace, but I still see the effects of the two doctrines as very similar. For those checking my orthodoxy, my personal belief is in original sin and prevenient grace.

having the law, are a law to themselves. [15] They show that what the law requires is written on their hearts, to which their own conscience also bears witness; and their conflicting thoughts will accuse or perhaps excuse them [16] on the day when, according to my gospel, God, through Jesus Christ, will judge the secret thoughts of all. — Romans 2:12-16 (NRSV)

This passage makes several additional points. First, according to verses 15 & 16, this knowledge is sufficient for one to take into judgment, and God may find the person acceptable. I think this denies certain concepts of original sin which suggest that there is no option for a person to come to understand God without the scriptures or some form of special revelation. (This is different from the requirement for prevenient grace.) Second, there is an interesting possible allusion to the law written on the heart (Jeremiah 31:33), a characteristic of the Messianic age. Third, it is apparent that one can follow the law instinctively.

If you look at a person's work product, you will see something of their nature.

To make this complete, to make each person without excuse, there must not only be the necessary information, but also the ability to make the choice. Either prevenient grace or a pelagian understanding of the will provide that element.

Other passages on the creation emphasize that the creation, the physical universe, results from God's word, from God's will and command. This suggests that we can learn a great deal about God simply from the way he has constructed the universe. I would suggest that Christians ignore this aspect of God's revelation too frequently

Let me suggest some questions:

1. What can we learn about God from nature?

2. What is the role of the Holy Spirit when we receive revelation?
3. Does the Holy Spirit always enlighten the mind of one who honestly seeks knowledge (a broadened, prevenient grace)?
4. How does the revelation of God in the natural world interact with direct or special revelation?

I want to suggest some answers, though I would hardly suggest these are firm conclusions.

LEARNING FROM NATURE

We can try to imagine the attributes of God that are reflected in his natural universe.

The things somebody makes definitely reflect something about that person. We can see this most clearly in art, but if you look at a person's work product, you will see something of their nature. At the same time, you will not learn everything about that person through the things they have made.

Supposing I write a computer program to do something fairly simple and straightforward, but it is something that many people want to do. Let's say that I do a really good job so quite a number of people use the program, and regard it as effective. They could conclude some things about me from looking at the program. First, I do know how to program a computer. (Note that in real life I haven't produced any substantial commercial successes!) Second, I was able to produce a program that accomplished something they wanted to accomplish. They could imagine from those observations that I'm a careful person who does good craftsmanship. (It would be hard, of course, for them to be certain that this single instance hadn't exhausted my capabilities.)

But they could also make some more questionable assumptions. They might assume that I was dedicated to the task performed by that particular program and thus had gone to an extraordinary effort to make sure people would be able to do that one thing. They might imagine me as a committed crusader, spending hours daily trying to carry out my crusade. Of course all that would ignore the possibility that I am a mercenary who desires lots of money and credit for my skills.

When we deal with the creation, we're in a similar position with God. We can look at the way the universe functions and we can see certain things about what is necessary to live in the universe. We can try to imagine the attributes of God that are reflected in his natural universe. These would include the law of cause and effect, and the apparent desire for creatures that have a range of freedom of action. Simple application of the law of cause and effect could make moral creatures of us, though we might choose rather different value systems.

But if God has a greater purpose for this world, this universe, and for our individual lives, the universe itself is not going to inform us. For that we would need special revelation if we are to know at all.

THE HOLY SPIRIT AND REVELATION

God's Holy Spirit enlightens everyone, and not just a select few.

It's easy to talk generally about the Holy Spirit and his involvement in revelation. We know that the Holy Spirit teaches us (John 14:26). The question is just what is that role? I will discuss this more later, but right now I simply want to suggest that the Holy Spirit is in the business of helping people pursue truth. There is no knowledge that is a prerequisite to having the Holy Spirit work in your life.

I combine the teaching role of the Holy Spirit with the basic freedom apparent in the universe to suggest that the Holy Spirit enlightens everyone to whatever extent they are willing to receive. Obviously this places me in direct opposition to the Calvinist position on predestination, yet it seems to combine the evident freedom of the universe and the experience of God quite nicely.

This same freedom suggests that God's Holy Spirit enlightens everyone, and not just a select few. Fairness would call for that. We have no way of being certain that God intends to be fair—just would be a more Biblical term—but the Bible does seem to suggest that he is. It seems difficult to me to combine fairness and partiality.

COMBINING GENERAL AND SPECIAL REVELATION

The role of each type of revelation seems obvious to me, provided that we simply look at how each functions. We look at nature and observe its facts. Facts of the physical world and explaining how they fit together are the province of scientific observation. We have repeated demonstrations of the effectiveness of this process in functioning technology, such as the computer and word processor I'm using to produce this book.

Facts of the physical world and explaining how they fit together are the province of scientific observation.

On the other hand, the *why* is not so clear from such observations. We can fit quite a number of different motivations and moral systems into the physical nature of the universe and the way in which our lives function in it. What is true? Here is where special revelation comes in.

There are two fairly obvious ways in which one can be misled, both of which result from applying the wrong type of revelation to the problem. Using special revelation to gain information about the physical world has resulted in young earth creationism, the doctrine that the earth (and the universe) is a mere 6,000 years old, and was created in six literal days. An overwhelming mass of scientific evidence stands against this conclusion. Everything we can learn from the natural world contradicts it, yet advocates hang onto it simply because they believe it is what the Bible teaches. The special revelation, in this case, trumps the revelation of the physical world in an area in which it should not.

The reverse case is Social Darwinism. Here simply because we observe that those most fit to fill an environmental niche will survive, while those less suited fail, we decide that in society this is what *ought* to be. In this case observations from science are abused to produce a moral conclusion.

DIRECT AND CLEAR REVELATION

I first truly struggled with this question in a small study group I was leading several years ago. Part of the group program was that we would take however much time the members wanted to and work through the meaning of each passage as long as the group cared to do so. This led to some rather lengthy arguments, and often to nitpicking the meaning. (You should only use this kind of approach in a study group if *everyone* truly wants to do it.) In one such session we were debating some passages in Revelation, and one of the members finally gave in to frustration and said, "Why can't God just write all this out in the sky clearly, so that we would know beyond any doubt what it meant?"

Why can't God just write all this out in the sky clearly, so that we would know beyond any doubt what it meant?

Hebrews 1:1-4 tells us that God has spoken at various times and in various ways *through the prophets*. Now, in the last days, he has spoken by means of his Son. But you and I still have to listen to God speak to someone else. We don't see a physical Jesus or hear him preach. Instead we read reports of what he said to other people 2,000 years ago. We don't even get to listen to the author of Hebrews; indeed, we can't seem to agree on who he (or some say she) is. So again we're hearing him speak to other people, and we are kind of eavesdropping. Why doesn't God make it clearer? Why doesn't he speak directly to me?

It's not just speaking directly, though. It's the clarity that's important. If God would just make the message personal, we would not have to consider just what the principles are, and how to apply them to our own lives–we'd know!

I believe that God does speak to each person directly, but clarity is another matter. In doing prayer ministry, one reason people will ask me to pray with them is that they *believe* they have heard from God, but they're not sure that it *is* God, or they're not sure just how to put it into practice.

This is not an easy question to resolve quickly, but it's a good question to think about. Let me make some suggestions:

1. **God wants us to learn to think.** We often treasure the work of the prophets, and we like the *results* of the wisdom writers, but are we willing to do the work that goes behind wisdom? Hebrews 5:14 tell us: "[14]Solid food is for the mature, for those who through practice have exercised their understanding to distinguish good and evil." God may well want us to practice our own judgment and discernment and grow in wisdom.

   God does speak to each person directly.

2. **God wants us to hear from him in a community.** Any one of us can go wildly astray on our own, but when we have accountability to brothers and sisters, at a minimum we have to consider the response of those close to us to what we say. Even writing a blog entry makes me give consideration to how people will receive and understand what I say. What impact will my words have? That is a natural accountability that comes simply from us being in community..

3. **God wants to leave us free to make unpressured decisions.** This is hard for some of us to understand, because we *think* we want to know and do precisely what God commands. But if God made himself too obvious, we might feel pressured just by his obvious presence, sort of like having the boss breathing down our neck.

4. **Those who actually listen to God are rare**. It's possible that God is speaking a great deal more than we are hearing, and that the prophets are the ones who listen more. If this one sounds good to you, make sure to consider the idea of the prophetic call Ezekiel 1 or Isaiah 6, for example, in this connection. Is it possible God calls many, and only a few hear and report the situation?

The Word was in the beginning; the Word was with God and the Word was God. Right at the beginning He was with God. All things came into existence through Him. – John 1:1-3a (HN)

THE WORD OF GOD

At some point, however, we are assuming that someone listens. For Abraham the word of God was something that God had spoken to him. We don't know how he discerned when God was speaking. Perhaps God graciously made it more clear to him, since he knew that Abraham had nothing to which he could compare what he heard.

> *God's word includes whatever God says, and since his word is also action, whatever God does.*

In modern times, the most common use of the phrase "word of God" is to refer to the written word, and specifically to that collection of books that we call the Bible. This is one case in which a change of terminology can be dangerous.

God's word includes whatever God says, and since his word is also action, whatever God does. The phrase word of God, as used in scripture, is very broad in meaning. The primary function of the word is creation. Genesis 1 emphasizes this and reemphasizes it by showing God speaking, and whatever God speaks, becomes so. Psalm 33:6-9 makes this explicit.

Psalm 104 first emphasizes the power of God's spoken Word (Psalm 104:7), and then the continuing nature of God's creative activity. Jesus is the Word made flesh (John 1:1-3; 14), the ultimate form of God's message to humanity (Hebrews 1:1-3).

Even salvation is an example of God's creative power in action, this time through the Word made flesh. "Anyone who belongs to Christ is a new person. The past is forgotten, and everything is new." - 2 Corinthians 5:17.

God created everything, and so we can learn about God from the natural world and the events that take place in it (general revelation). While we cannot get the same information from studying nature that we can through God's revealed Word in scripture (special revelation) and through the gift of prophecy, we can get truth which comes from studying the word of God in action.

When we engage in scientific study truthfully and honestly, we are studying the word of God.

When we engage in scientific study truthfully and honestly, we are studying the word of God. We can approach it with prayer, reverence, and an openness to what God wants us to learn. We should certainly approach it with honesty.

There are some who suggest that we should study the natural world specifically to support certain theological presuppositions. But the best way to learn accurately about God in his creation is by observing it as objectively as possible. We need to allow nature to speak to us just as we allow the scriptures to speak with us, and allow both to correct our own understanding. Together they will bring us a more complete picture of our creator.

But while creation is the primary function of the word, the physical things that are created are not the sole way in which we can receive the word. In the past God has spoken to us in many ways. He has sent angels (Genesis 18), He has spoken directly (Genesis 22, Exodus 19:16-25). He has given visions (Ezekiel 1, Isaiah 6, Acts 10) and dreams (Matthew 2:19-20), and communicated through through direct prophetic utterances.

Many of these are recorded in the Bible and throughout Christian history. The chart below presents a general process by which the word of God is received:

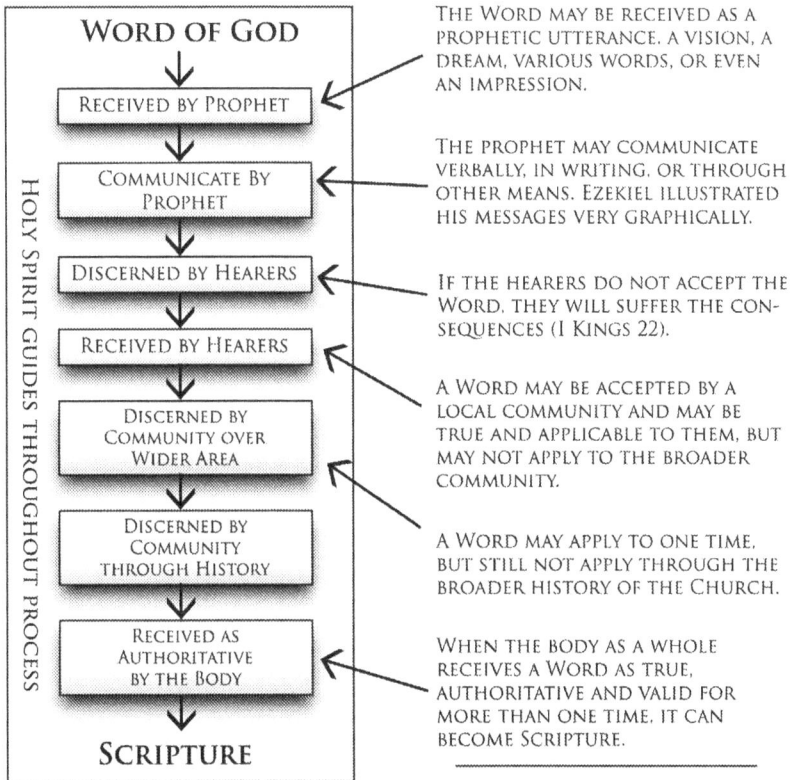

WORD OF GOD ↓ RECEIVED BY PROPHET ↓ COMMUNICATE BY PROPHET ↓ DISCERNED BY HEARERS ↓ RECEIVED BY HEARERS ↓ DISCERNED BY COMMUNITY OVER WIDER AREA ↓ DISCERNED BY COMMUNITY THROUGH HISTORY ↓ RECEIVED AS AUTHORITATIVE BY THE BODY ↓ **SCRIPTURE**	THE WORD MAY BE RECEIVED AS A PROPHETIC UTTERANCE, A VISION, A DREAM, VARIOUS WORDS, OR EVEN AN IMPRESSION. THE PROPHET MAY COMMUNICATE VERBALLY, IN WRITING, OR THROUGH OTHER MEANS. EZEKIEL ILLUSTRATED HIS MESSAGES VERY GRAPHICALLY. IF THE HEARERS DO NOT ACCEPT THE WORD, THEY WILL SUFFER THE CONSEQUENCES (1 KINGS 22). A WORD MAY BE ACCEPTED BY A LOCAL COMMUNITY AND MAY BE TRUE AND APPLICABLE TO THEM, BUT MAY NOT APPLY TO THE BROADER COMMUNITY. A WORD MAY APPLY TO ONE TIME, BUT STILL NOT APPLY THROUGH THE BROADER HISTORY OF THE CHURCH. WHEN THE BODY AS A WHOLE RECEIVES A WORD AS TRUE, AUTHORITATIVE AND VALID FOR MORE THAN ONE TIME, IT CAN BECOME SCRIPTURE.

(Left margin label: HOLY SPIRIT GUIDES THROUGHOUT PROCESS)

THE WORD OF GOD MUST STILL BE RECEIVED BY THE INDIVIDUAL READER THROUGH THE POWER OF THE HOLY SPIRIT, AND APPLIED IN ONE'S LIFE.

THROUGHOUT THIS PROCESS GOD'S WORD IS ALWAYS GOD'S WORD AND IS TRUE. THE QUESTION IS ALWAYS IN DISCERNING THAT IT IS GOD'S WORD AND IN RECEIVING IT.

God Speaks - 31

THE PROCESS OF REVELATION

The process of revelation often involves many steps and many people, especially if the message to you comes through scripture. Often we ignore parts of this process, but every step is important, and it has an impact on how we will understand what we read.

- ✔ Someone must receive the Word from the Lord.

- ✔ Listeners must then receive that communication as a Word. Without the inspiration of the listeners, the Word cannot become scripture.

- ✔ It must then be passed to the broader community-other churches, synagogues or other centers of worship.

The process of revelation often involves many steps and many people.

- ✔ It must be found to be applicable over a long period of time.

- ✔ There is no single set of characteristics of the original writing. A great variety of types of literature have become scripture. Some of the historical books of the Bible, such as Kings and Chronicles, bear evidence that they were written based on existing chronicles. The writer researched, compiled and organized his material.

All of this happens under the guidance of the Holy Spirit.

When the body of Christ (the church universal) receives a written text as authoritative, then it becomes what we call scripture. This process is called canonization. No single group or denomination can make new scripture. They may have Word(s) from the Lord, but those do not have the authority of the Bible without the acceptance of the whole body.

There are many caricatures of what happens in the collection of scripture. On the one extreme we have those who believe that the apostles themselves sat down, examined all the writings available, and chose what would be scriptures. On the other extreme we have those who picture the church councils, complete with various conspirators gathering in isolated rooms, and deciding which writings would best support their own position of power.

In fact, canonization occurred as the people of God recognized works as authoritative because they used them in many places and over a long period of time. The councils largely simply accepted what the Holy Spirit had already accomplished through the individual churches.

ALL TRUTH COMES FROM THE WORD.

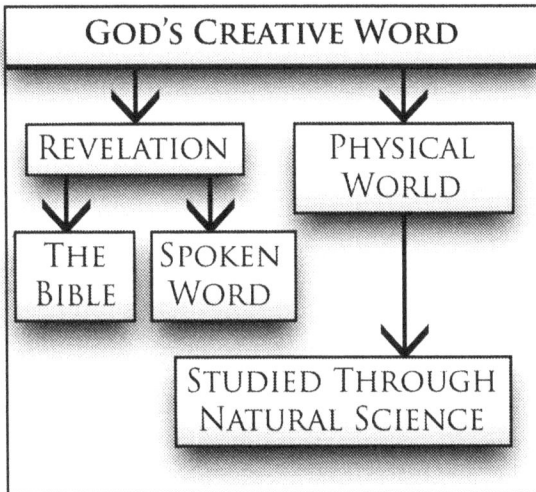

Think of this as multiple processes involved in the revelation of scripture, with God involved in every one.

- ✔ God communicates with the prophet
- ✔ God communicates with the ancient community to whom the prophet is called as a messenger
- ✔ God communicates with the modern community
- ✔ God communicates with the broad Christian community throughout time
- ✔ The writer or speaker of God's word is communicating with his audience
- ✔ The writer or speaker of the word is communicating with us

God not only has information for us; he has a plan.

Our tendency is to look just at the message of the text itself, but all of these elements can help us understand how God works in the world. When you add to that the recorded actions of God through the Bible, you have another method of coming to understand God better. My goal in writing this book is to encourage you to think about and learn from all of the ways in which God acts.

ALIVE AND ACTIVE

> *[12]For the word {message} of God is alive and active, sharper than any two edged sword, piercing to the division of the soul and spirit, bones and marrow, and judging the desires and thoughts of the heart {mind}. [13]And there is no creature who is not visible to him, for everything is naked and laid bare to his eyes, to whom we must render an account. — Hebrews 4:12-13 (HN)*

Yes, but what does it do? The primary function of the word of God is creation. Its present focus, in all of its forms, is to create new people from you and me.

I sometimes think that this passage should be our key passage for the inspiration of the Bible rather than 2 Timothy 3:16. After opening with the wonderful passage in Hebrews 1:1-4, and telling us how God has communicated in so many ways, the author of Hebrews begins to close the circle on the Word of God, and the powerful work that it does. The word came in many ways at many different times, but now it has come through a Son, Jesus Christ. This word challenges us to its quality and nature (Hebrews 2:1-4). God not only has information for us; he has a plan. We don't only need to know the contents; we need to let our lives reflect that content. When we "consider the apostle and high priest of our confession" it is not so that we can polish up our doctrinal statements, it is so that we will be faithful to our confession.

Hebrews 4:12-13 brings a close to this part of the argument and launches us into a new phase as we discuss priesthood. To catch the emphasis, let me translate very literally: "Living is the Word of God and active/powerful . . ." There has been some debate over whether our author here is talking about Jesus (John 1:1-3) as the word, or is talking about the scriptures. Scholarly opinion centers on the second. But I think both are too narrow. I think he has seen the marvelous ways in which God, through his word, intrudes himself into our lives. He sees the benefits that will result from responding to this activity and makes a call for us to be faithful to that call.

The word is active, and we need to get active with the word.

That's why the next section of this passage talks about knowledge. God's word not only enlightens us and informs us, it discovers all that there is to be known about us. You can get a picture almost of dissection, but that wasn't on our author's mind. He was probably looking more at a combat metaphor of the skilled swordsman whose sword finds the precise mark. But in this case the purpose is not to wound, but to lay it all bare before the eyes of God. All creation is open to him because, after all, he is the creator of everything. It's all laid bare.

The word of God is both **in**formative and formative. It provides us with knowledge of God. It is God, who knows all there is to know about us. It is the motivator of our actions and the empowerment to do them.

> *By the word of YHWH the heavens were made,*
> *By the breath of his mouth, all their host! — Psalm*
> *33:6 (HN)*

But then perhaps 2 Timothy 3:16 is not so far off after all. In fact, as I read it, I see much the same thing. "Every scripture is God-breathed, and is useful for teaching, for rebuke, for correction (straightening out), and for instruction in righteousness." Isn't that pretty much what this is saying? I find that this verse gets quoted more often to tell us what the content of scripture is. The Greek term "theopneustos" (God-breathed) is analyzed to tell us how inspiration works, and what it must do to the words of scripture. In fact, the Revised English Bible translates, "All inspired scripture has its use . . ." and many people have told me that this takes all meaning from the verse. Not at all! What Paul is getting at here is how to put the scripture to practical use. **The word is active, and we need to get active with the word.** We need to let the word change us.

When that sword cut to the heart of the matter, what did it find?

One particularly important point I like to emphasize in Bible study is the need to let the word correct you personally first. It is so easy to read the Bible, or hear the word in any context, and find all of the things that other people need to hear. There is correction there for my wife, for my children, for my pastor, for my Sunday School class. But the real question is this: When that sword cut to the heart of the matter, what did it find?

That should be the focus of our Bible study!

STATIC, PROGRESSIVE, OR CONTINUOUS?

Christians frequently claim to follow every word of the Bible. That is said with an air of piety that suggests that all true Christians, will, of course, follow everything that the Bible says.

But I know when I hear this that someone either hasn't been reading the Bible very carefully or hasn't been thinking about it very clearly. Generally I can ask very simple questions to get someone to acknowledge that they do not, in fact, follow every word. For example, if you are a Christian, do you offer animal sacrifices? No? Why not? It's a command of scripture.

You will probably answer that for various reasons that command doesn't apply to us any more, and that's precisely the point. There are things in scripture that are commanded for a specific time, person, or place. We generally don't get those too confused. When Moses is told to drop his rod on the ground so that it becomes a snake (Exodus 4:3), nobody is tempted to start a ritual of staff dropping, because we all know that the command was for one person. Other commands are much more controversial.

"An eye for an eye" moved the people in the direction in which God wanted them to go, but it did not express God's ideal.

One response to this is the idea of progressive revelation. God has revealed more and more over time, expanding our understanding of him, and thus later revelation can override earlier revelation. An illustration of this type of approach can be found in the Sermon on the Mount.

> *38 You know that you have been taught, "An eye for an eye and a tooth for a tooth." 39 But I tell you not to try to get even with a person who has done something to you. When someone slaps your right cheek, turn and let that person slap your other cheek. 40 If someone sues you for your shirt, give up your coat as well. 41 If*

a soldier forces you to carry his pack one mile, carry it
two miles. [42] *When people ask you for something, give*
it to them. When they want to borrow money, lend it to
them. — Matthew 5:38-42 (CEV)

Note that the command "an eye for an eye and a tooth for a tooth"
comes from the Bible, one instance being Exodus 21:24-25. Under
progressive revelation, we would understand this to be a command
that was appropriate at the time, and possibly as much as the people
could take. It moved them in the direction in which God wanted
them to go, but it did not express God's ideal.

It is typical of later religions to make a claim that their own newer revelation is greater than what has gone before. Though in the modern world we view "an eye for an eye" as a terribly barbaric standard, yet when it was first enacted in the ancient near east, its intention was to limit revenge, not to prescribe it. (See below on trajectories, page 53.)

To look at this in a broader way, one of the key themes of the book of Hebrews is that Jesus is a greater revelation than that provided by the Torah. In order to support this claim, the author must first establish that revelation is in some sense progressive, though he does not develop a doctrine of progressive revelation, but rather establishes that a new, greater revelation can supersede an earlier one.

This is a key difference between Christianity and Judaism. Judaism sees the Torah as the ultimate revelation, and everything that follows is less authoritative. The idea of something appearing that would supersede the Torah is pretty much anathema. It is typical of later religions to make a claim that their own newer revelation is greater than what has gone before. For Christianity, it's Jesus and the New Testament, but then many Christians want to claim that revelation has ceased. For Islam (or at least the vast majority of it), the Qur'an is the final revelation, and cannot be superseded. It's finally the perfect thing.

But Christians divide on this point, some believing in one form or another of continuing revelation, while others believe that revelation ceased with the age of the apostles. Amongst Christians, liberals and charismatics tend to see revelation as continuing, while the reformed movement and those related to it see revelation as complete with the Bible. There are a number of special cases, such as the Roman Catholic church and the concept of the "magisterium." The "magisterium" is the teaching function of the church which applies scripture to particular times and places. It functions very much like continuing revelation, though technically it is not. The Latter Day Saints have their living apostles who can bring out new revelation.

I have often wondered how Isaiah, Jeremiah, and Ezekiel would fare if we had as detailed a record of their lives, along with copies of every letter they ever wrote.

I grew up as Seventh-day Adventist, and one of the key controversies between Seventh-day Adventists and the rest of the Christian community is over Ellen White. Can you have a modern prophet, and how does this relate to scripture? Here again I think there is a difference in the way things are expressed and the way they are put into practice. My experience was that many Adventists used the writings of Ellen White as though they were scripture, no matter how church doctrine was stated. But I don't think Seventh-day Adventists are alone on this issue. The place of the prophetic movement in charismatic and pentecostal churches is very similar and I see some of the same things being done either with words from the Lord, visions, and writings. Some conversation here between modern charismatics and Seventh-day Adventists might be valuable.

Often modern prophets are criticized for their mistakes or for various problems in their personal lives. There is a key difference between the way in which we examine a modern prophet, and the way we look at an ancient one. First, we give the ancient prophet the benefit of any doubt. We don't look at Ezekiel, for example, and question whether he really was a prophet, yet people in the past did just that. Second, we have so much more material available. Ellen White (Seventh-day Adventist Church), for example, left stacks of letters, papers and notes, and there are hundreds of witnesses to her life. Everything that she said, wrote, and did is involved in criticizing her and her mission. We have no such records for Biblical prophets.

I have often wondered how Isaiah, Jeremiah, and Ezekiel would fare if we had as detailed a record of their lives, along with copies of every letter they ever wrote. For better or worse, we don't get to compare the first draft of Jeremiah with the second, and even attempts at a chronology of his message are often quite speculative.

When God tells Jeremiah to write down these words, it is not a new revelation.

Yet there is some indication that things are not as calm as they seem at first glance. We do have more than one version of the book. The LXX (Septuagint) translation of Jeremiah is about 10% longer than that of the Masoretic (Hebrew) text. At one point this was thought to be because of loose translation on the part of the LXX translators, but more recently some support for LXX readings has been found in the Dead Sea Scrolls. This suggests that there were either two different transmitted texts, resulting from a copyist, or it is even possible that Jeremiah produced two different versions within his own lifetime. We certainly have some basis for considering that possibility.

Jeremiah 36 starts with God's command to Jeremiah to have a scroll written containing his prophecies, the words he had received from the Lord:

> *During the fourth year that Jehoiakim son of Josiah was king of Judah, the LORD said to me, "Jeremiah, ² since the time Josiah was king, I have been speaking to you about Israel, Judah, and the other nations. Now,*

get a scroll and write down everything I have told you,
³ then read it to the people of Judah. Maybe they will
stop sinning when they hear what terrible things I plan
for them. And if they turn to me, I will forgive them."

⁴ I sent for Baruch son of Neriah and asked him to help
me. I repeated everything the LORD had told me, and
Baruch wrote it all down on a scroll. — Jeremiah
36:1-4

It's important to notice here that when God tells Jeremiah to write down these words, it is not a new revelation. The revelation had already been given orally and proclaimed to various people. There is also no indication in the text that God is going to dictate these words to Jeremiah again.

Then Jeremiah feels free to get help. He doesn't personally write the revelation on the scroll, but instead had Baruch write it.

Be assured that a call to be a prophet is not a call to power, fun, and long life!

But this revelation is not entirely appreciated by the audience. It eventually finds its way to the king. Here's his response:

²⁰⁻²² The officials put the scroll in Elishama's room
and went to see the king, who was in one of the rooms
where he lived and worked during the winter. It was
the ninth month of the year, so there was a fire burning
in the fireplace, and the king was sitting nearby. After
the officials told the king about the scroll, he sent
Jehudi to get it. Then Jehudi started reading the scroll
to the king and his officials. ²³⁻²⁵ But every time Jehudi
finished reading three or four columns, the king would
tell him to cut them off with his penknife and throw
them in the fire. Elnathan, Delaiah, and Gemariah

begged the king not to burn the scroll, but he ignored them, and soon there was nothing left of it. — Jeremiah 36:20-25

So the original copy of Jeremiah's words gets burned, which is not an uncommon fate for the words of a prophet. Be assured that a call to be a prophet is not a call to power, fun, and long life!

But Jeremiah is not stopped by this fate to his words. God tells him to produce another scroll like the first one.

²⁷ I had told Baruch what to write on that first scroll, but King Jehoiakim had burned it. So the LORD told me ²⁸ to get another scroll and write down everything that had been on the first one. — Jeremiah 36:27-28

"Progressive revelation" has gotten tangled with the same types of misunderstandings that are involved in biological evolution.

Such a process could result in a text of slightly differing length, and it's quite possible that there were other times in Jeremiah's life when he dictated portions of his message more than once. All of that is speculation, but it does show that it is *possible* that there could even have been more than one *autograph* of Jeremiah.

Now that we have seen that the composition of the Bible is not so smooth as one might suppose, let's return to the idea of new revelation. We have seen that there is good Biblical evidence for *new* revelation, but is revelation generally progressive? Can a new revelation override an old one?

"Progressive" is a terribly dangerous word. In biology, evolution is often described as a progress from simple to complex, primitive to modern, with "modern" defined as "better." As time goes forward some suppose that organisms become better adapted to their environment, so that we have a constant movement toward perfection. But if you read descriptions of evolution by actual biologists, this picture doesn't seem to work quite as well. One can say for certain that variety has generally increased, there is more diversity now than there was in the Cambrian period, but none of the other claims I mentioned can be made with certainty. "More complex" may mean *less* adapted, and thus natural selection would select for simplicity. The environment changes as well, so one cannot be certain that we're always moving to better adaptation.

Why bring biological evolution in here? Simply because progressive revelation is often compared to biological evolution, especially in a negative sense. Some scientists and even Biblical scholars are accused of applying evolution to everything, and this is used as an example. Well, one can certain apply some evolutionary concepts to anything that changes, but that's not really the issue here. "Progressive revelation" has gotten tangled with the same types of misunderstandings that are involved in biological evolution. First, it is assumed that any new revelation must automatically supersede an older revelation. Second, it is assumed that as time goes on the revelation we have in our possession will be better and better, so that we will become closer and closer to the truth about God.

The revelation is not, in fact, adapting itself.

Just as the inevitable progress of biological evolution does not seem so well founded, and just as adaptation can go on for many millions of years without any assurance that anything actually gets 100% adapted, so I see little reason to assume that revelation will always get better and better. What I personally hear from the Lord is more adapted to my circumstances. A current revelation to a church community will be better adapted to their time and their place, but because we are imperfect people, we will always have problems fully comprehending that revelation. A perfect revelation cannot be 100% adapted to imperfect recipients.

Let's refer back to the one-ended telephone cord. We can only comment on the quality of revelation by also noting how well that revelation is understood. God's communication with various individuals could easily be different.

But my prior paragraph could easily be misunderstood. The biological analogy breaks down. The revelation is not, in fact, adapting itself. Rather, the revelation is coming to different people, in different circumstances, at different times, and in different ways. It has always been that way. We can refine our understanding, but again, because we are imperfect, there is no guarantee that we are always getting better. We can *hope* we are, but we cannot be certain. The next generation could look back at our time and laugh, just as many of us laugh at a prior time.

This increase in quantity and variety gives me an advantage. I think that God is continually revealing himself, continually speaking. We hear with varied clarity. In scripture and established traditions, we take those things that have been heard, confirmed, and reaffirmed at many times and in many places. What Isaiah said is not necessarily better than what someone hears from the Lord in their morning devotions. But Isaiah's words have been used and tested repeatedly by many people over a long period of our tradition, and so have been accepted as of genuine, general value over a wide geographic area and over a broad range of times. The fact that his book is scripture is a definition of the community that accepts it, not a simple derivation from the nature of the content.

I know there will be those who are disturbed. I am overcome by delusions of grandeur, and am receiving revelations of the quality and value of those of the prophet Isaiah. [Pause for effect :-)] Well, no, I'm not. But if God speaks to me, and if I hear correctly, the words of God are just as true whispered in my ear as in anybody else's. And of course they are just as true whispered in anybody else's ear, including the ear of someone I despise, as they are in mine.

I have more options to test these words now because I have scripture, as defined by my community, and I can even dabble in scripture as defined by other communities just to compare. This increase in quantity and variety gives me an advantage. One pictures Abraham, as tradition suggests, dealing with idols as was the family business, and suddenly addressed by God. "Get out of here! Go somewhere that I'll show you!" Abraham has very little to go on. Scripture doesn't exist yet, and won't for centuries. He simply has to decide whether to accept what the voice says (presumably based on the patriarchal tradition, but do *you* want to decide on God's voice based on *your* family tradition?) or not. I have it easier. I have a community; I'm not about to found one. I have other people who at least claim to hear God speak, though this is often more of a hindrance than otherwise. There's more variety.

All of the ways in which we can determine just what inspiration means are circular to some extent.

But fundamentally God speaking is God speaking, and I don't think it's getting better or worse. We just have more instances of it to study. Thus I prefer the term "continuous" over "progressive."

THE HEART OF INSPIRATION

So what is the heart of inspiration? What do people generally mean when they say that something written is inspired by God? There are many different answers to this question. Some options are:

✔ God gave the very words and letters of the work in question This would apply to the Ten Commandments written on tablets of stone by God's finger, to the Torah according to many Orthodox Jews, or to the entire Bible according to some conservative or fundamentalist Christians who believe in verbal dictation. Only those things God dictated would be regarded as inspired.

- ✔ God impresses messages on the minds of certain people, who write those messages in their own words. Many conservative and moderate Christians hold a view like this. There is room for the personality of the prophet, and there is room for individual idiosyncrasies, but there must be a specific message sent by God.
- ✔ People who experience God try to describe what they have experienced.

  This is a common liberal view of the inspiration of scripture. It is quite possible for there to be errors in scripture, but those who write do have a genuine experience of God. The validity of their descriptions may vary.

The core of an inspired writing is that the person doing the writing, or producing the information, has genuinely experienced God in some way.

There are different ways one can use to decide what inspiration means. All of these will be circular to some extent. For example, many people build their view of inspiration almost entirely from their understanding of the nature of God. God is all-knowing and truthful, so the Bible must be factually accurate and entirely truthful. This is the approach taken by those who believe in inerrancy. It has also been used in my experience by Muslims who have tried to persuade me that the Qur'an is the word of God. Others look heavily at human needs, and make the assumption that divine revelation would necessarily fill in what we don't know and can't know. There is a consistent assumption that God is intending to communicate knowledge to us, and knowledge that is absolutely accurate.

In either case, these people will take either the first or second view that I present about inspiration. The process is primarily about conveying information and the primary question to be asked is whether the information conveyed is accurate and comprehensible. I think that their view works fairly well for books that at least appear to claim to come from God. Isaiah, Jeremiah, and Ezekiel claimed to be receiving messages from God and to write these messages. But what about other books? Luke claims to be writing the results of research. Samuel, Kings, and Chronicles appear to be history, and find their source in previously existing royal chronicles. Psalms contains prayers that are individual, and seem to express the heart cry of the individual psalmist.

I would argue instead for the third view. My problem is not that the other views are circular, and that my alternative is not. It is inevitable that when we talk about revelation, something revealed by God that we could not otherwise know, we're going to get a bit circular. After all, how do we know it is God talking? If the information is readily available to us, we can learn it from a natural source and test it by natural means. If the information is not available to us, naturally, what standard can we use to test it?

Yet You have made him a little lower than God, And You crown him with glory and majesty! — Psalm 8:5 (NASB95)

If you accept the third view, then the other books I have cited fall into place. There are many ways in which God speaks, many ways in which we can hear, and many ways in which we can express what we hear. That experience may come through direct impression of messages from God in the mind, visions, dreams, guided study, or even guided experiencing of the world. The Biblical writer experiences God's presence and records it in his own way..

The core, then, of an inspired writing is that the person doing the writing, or producing the information, has genuinely experienced God in some way.

INSPIRATION IN ACTION: AN EXAMPLE

We can see inspiration in action in the book of Hebrews. A good example is Hebrews 2:6-9, and particularly verse 7, quoted from Psalm 8:5 (all verse numbers from the English Bible, Psalm 8:5 is 8:6

in Hebrew). Now this quotation is an excellent example of a couple of translation problems, and though that is not my purpose here, I need to outline them in support of my major point.

First, there is the issue of translation in Psalm 8:5. Translations split between reading "a little lower than the angels/heavenly beings" or "a little lower than God/the gods/a god." It's interesting that mainstream to liberal translations such as the New Revised Standard Version (NRSV) and Revised English Bible(REB) find themselves in at least partial agreement with the very conservative New American Standard Bible (NASB) on this issue. (The NASB's "than God" is a little less jarring to Christian ears than the REB's "little less than a god," perhaps, but both tend in the same direction.)

An author would grab hold of his favorite tool and apply it to every scripture in sight.

In Hebrews, you will find the quotation consistently translated as "lower than the angels" or something quite close to that. The reason for the consistency in Hebrews is quite simple. The quotation is from the LXX (Septuagint), which translated this passage as "angels."

The other translation issue of note is whether to translate the Greek "βραχυ/brachu" as "for a little while" or "a little." The Greek word could possibly handle either interpretation, but the context and grammar tends to suggest "a little while." Some translations, such as the New International Version (NIV), try to accommodate the two translations, using "a little lower" in Hebrews 2:7, and keeping the translation as consistent as possible with Psalm 8:5, but adding a footnote to the alternate translation. Others, such as the NASB and the NRSV again simply translate the text of Hebrews without concern for consistency with Psalm 8:5.

Note here that I'm just making note of these translation choices, not criticizing any of them. With very little work I could justify the actions of each translation team, and considering that alternatives are indicated in footnotes in many cases, I have no problem. What I do want you to see is that there are a couple of differences between the LXX text as quoted by the author of Hebrews, and the Hebrew text as we have in our Old Testaments. And that's why this particular verse caught my eye.

One of the things that got me thinking when I first started looking at the tools of Biblical criticism, especially form and source criticism, was that an author would grab hold of his favorite tool and apply it to every scripture in sight willy-nilly, and with interesting results. Many times the main objections to the use of a critical tool could be eliminated by carefully defining the tool itself and the types of texts on which it could be effective, and then carefully applying that tool only in those places.

> *The fact that the author of Genesis did put the two chapters together suggests that to him they were not contradictory.*

But there was a further problem. Even in the case of texts in which a particular tool applied, many students would use just the one tool and then be done with it. For example, in studying Isaiah, one might use form criticism to define the boundaries and structure of a prophetic oracle, then define it down to a subcategory of oracle, place it in the appropriate setting, and come up with a plausible (hopefully!) understanding of what Isaiah intended when presenting that oracle orally to its original audience. A person dedicated to form criticism as a method of interpretation would stop there. The study of the book of Isaiah was simply a study of a series of oracles. The book itself tended to disappear.

Another example comes from Genesis 1 & 2, which have some contradictions or apparent contradictions (I don't care which for the moment) in terms of the chronology of creation. Someone applying source criticism might simply respond to these problems by stating that the two chapters come from different sources, and consider the question answered. But we are left with the question of why an apparently intelligent person (and anyone who has studied the literary structure of Genesis must concede that its author is intelligent) would put the two chapters together with content that appears so obviously contradictory to us. Either we see "contradictory" in very different terms, he doesn't really care about contradiction, or we're missing something. The fact that he *did* put the two chapters together suggests that *to him* they were not contradictory. That doesn't mean that he may not have had two creation story sources or traditions in front of him as he wrote. It does mean that he understood those sources as compatible and thought that each had a message that would contribute to the book he was compiling.

We are heavily trained by our modern, scientific approach to information to look for the source, for the original meaning, for the oldest form. Many of these problems have been alleviated considerably by the use of such methods as canonical and genre criticism. A good example of the use of canonical criticism is Brevard Childs' commentary on Isaiah (OTL).[5] I would note, however, that this canonical approach to criticism has by no means won the field. Much of the work on the historical Jesus, especially that of the Jesus Seminar, is heavily based on the approach of form criticism, whether that is admitted or not. The starting point for Jesus Seminar material is in breaking the text into blocks on which the analysis is performed to determine just how authentic a particular saying or event is. As oral material–Jesus himself didn't write it down–the sayings of Jesus are well suited to study through form criticism. But is such study all we need to do?[6]

Let's return to Hebrews 2:6-9. I think it is clear that the author of Hebrews is getting a somewhat different point from Psalm 8 than was actually intended by the original author for his audience. Psalm 8 celebrates God, and the position of humanity in God's creation.

---

5   Childs, Brevard. Isaiah (Old Testament Library). Philadelphia: Westminster John Knox Press, 2000.

6   Compare The Five Gospels with Darrell Bock's Jesus According to Scripture to see both methods in action clearly.

Hebrews 2 uses that passage either as a prophecy or a type of Jesus, who is made lower than the angels for his earthly ministry, and then crowned with glory and honor afterward. My modern mind can get a little twisted with that. After all, the author is not doing exegesis, at least not such as would get an 'A' grade in seminary. He's using the wording of the text in a slightly different way than it was intended. What's more, assuming that since he seems to translate loosely himself in some places, and may well have had the Hebrew text available to him, he is *cherry picking* his translation to suit his message! What's up with that?

In my view, he is permitted to do this because he was *inspired*. We are heavily trained by our modern, scientific approach to information to look for the source, for the original meaning, for the oldest form. (However much we talk about postmodern, most of the public still has a more "modern" view, I believe.) Because of this bias we are quite susceptible to the claims of certain critical methods. Form and source criticism will get us closer to the original. Who wouldn't want that? The methods are challenged primarily on the basis of results— they didn't get us to where we thought they would. But the basic idea of finding the oldest form is something with which we are very comfortable.

> *It's interesting to hear people claim that the early Christians quickly corrupted the teachings of Jesus and at the same time assume that they can extract the true story from a distance of millenia.*

GOD THROUGHOUT THE PROCESS

Perhaps we would do better to ask "Where *didn't* God act?" The question people have most commonly is precisely how God is involved, but as with the world, God is involved everywhere. At each point in the process that brings God's word to you, God must be involved.

I'm confident that Isaiah made prophetic utterances orally. I'm confident that they were later written down and collected, and that they were finally shaped into the book as we have it today. As authority in the church, we accept the *book* of Isaiah, because that is *canonical*, that is, it is is what we have officially made authoritative. But from the historical point of view, and also based on my interest in knowing how God has worked with people throughout history, I'm interested in the whole process, because that tells me something about God.

I don't mind the search for the historical Jesus. I'm interested in precisely what Jesus said. But from the practical point of view isn't it somewhat odd to try to filter out the voices of the first century Christians who wrote down and collected what Jesus said, and those who shaped the result into gospels, in favor of filtering purely through my own mind? While I do want to know precisely what Jesus said (though I'll have to wait until the kingdom to *actually* know), I suspect the filter of the early Christians is actually more reliable than my own. It's interesting to hear people claim that the early Christians quickly corrupted the teachings of Jesus and at the same time assume that they can extract the true story from a distance of millenia with a high degree of confidence.

We tend to look down on the compiler, the copyist, and those involved in determining canonicity, by comparison with an original author.

I think it's perfectly valid for the author of Psalm 8 to make one point, and the author of Hebrews to use his words to make another. In fact, I think those points are typologically related. Where did God speak? Well, he spoke in Genesis, which was probably in the mind of the Psalmist as he wrote. He spoke in Psalms 8, which is a wonderfully encouraging passage. He spoke again through both the words and deeds of Jesus, especially his death, resurrection, and exaltation at the side of the Father. He spoke again through the author of Hebrews who points us to the change of status that Jesus accepted, and who provides an interpretation of those actions for us.

I believe God speaks in all these things, and that we can get valuable insights from the whole experience of God's action in the world. Hebrews 2:6-9 gives us a snapshot of inspiration in action.

TRAJECTORIES

I like to talk about trajectories in scripture. This may sound odd to some. A trajectory, according to Merriam-Webster, is "a path, progression, or line of development resembling a physical trajectory." When I talk about scriptural trajectories, I'm referring in particular to the last part of that definition–a line of development.

Many Biblical passages need to be read not simply to find out what the say, and who they are saying it to, but also to discover where God is going with a particular set of commands. This connects very closely to the some issues I have already discussed, such as the progressive or continuous nature of revelation, and seeing value in the entire process.

Before the "eye for an eye" rule, vengeance was according to the desires of the avenger.

If the people who wrote the Bible experienced the presence of God, then it seems just as likely to me that the people who collected and editing the material also have an experience of God, and so do those involved in canonization. We tend to look down on the compiler, the copyist, and those involved in determining canonicity, by comparison with an original author, but is there a good reason to do so? Is there any reason they cannot all partake of God's inspiration, God's breath in their lives?

In Christian theology we might identify a trajectory in a tabernacle and a sacrificial system that leads eventually to direct, personal access to God's throne as described in the book of Hebrews. The command to offer a lamb might seem to merely indicate that God likes animal sacrifices. If we view it in the light of the trajectory, we may find that

God does not like sin, and likes us to be reminded of it each time. In addition, it can remind us of the cost of sin on a regular basis, and also tell us that even if we are very far from God, he is nonetheless willing to make a way for us to approach him.

In this case the trajectory also helps us get at the core of meaning in the original text and ritual. What was God's ultimate intent with the sacrificial system? The best way to answer this question is to look at what actually happened to it in scripture as we know it now.

The sacrificial system can tell us that even if we are very far from God, he is nonetheless willing to make a way for us to approach him.

Another trajectory in scripture is the view of vengeance. We often see "an eye for an eye and a tooth for a tooth" (Leviticus 24:19-20) as an illustration of barbaric punishment, set aside by Jesus in favor of forgiveness. But I like to picture these points on a graph and then ask where they're going. Before the "eye for an eye" rule, vengeance was according to the desires of the avenger. Some of the results of that can be seen in Genesis 34 with the disproportionate revenge of Dinah's brothers (Jacob's sons) to action taken against their sister. If we move forward from that to God's claim to be the only true avenger (Deuteronomy 32:35 as quoted in Romans 12:19), we are tracking a Biblical trajectory.

I want to illustrate this concept briefly from Numbers 35:9-29, the command to establish cities of refuge. Observe the bolded passages especially:

> *9 The LORD spoke to Moses, saying: 10 Speak to the Israelites, and say to them: When you cross the Jordan into the land of Canaan, 11 then you shall select cities to be cities of refuge for you, so that a slayer who kills a person without intent may flee there. 12 The cities shall be for you a refuge from the avenger, so that the*

slayer may not die until there is a trial before the congregation.

If we see the starting point of this trajectory as a situation where revenge is an individual matter and people return multiples of the evil that people have done to them. Feuds are made of this kind of revenge, in which a series of vengeance killings doesn't end because it never appears to be balanced. Within that trajectory we move to "an eye for an eye" as we've discussed earlier, and then in this passage we encounter the innocent person who has harmed somebody by accident.

I want you to think now of how you would normally resolve this situation today. Most of us will agree that a person who injures or kills someone totally by accident should not be executed. Yet that is not the solution provided here. The solution is, however, much better than simply allowing personal revenge, even under the "eye for an eye" principle, technically called *lex talionis.*

> *Most of us will agree that a person who injures or kills someone totally by accident should not be executed.*

13 The cities that you designate shall be six cities of refuge for you: 14 you shall designate three cities beyond the Jordan, and three cities in the land of Canaan, to be cities of refuge. 15 These six cities shall serve as refuge for the Israelites, for the resident or transient alien among them, so that anyone who kills a person without intent may flee there.

At the rate of travel of someone fleeing, a person might take a day or two to arrive at the city of refuge. During the time he was running, he could be killed. That is the point of his fleeing.

16 But anyone who strikes another with an iron object, and death ensues, is a murderer; the murderer shall be put to death. 17 Or anyone who strikes another with a stone in hand that could cause death, and death ensues, is a murderer; the murderer shall be put to death. 18 Or anyone who strikes another with a weapon of wood in hand that could cause death, and death ensues, is a murderer; the murderer shall be put to death. 19 The avenger of blood is the one who shall put the murderer to death; when they meet, the avenger of blood shall execute the sentence. 20 Likewise, if someone pushes another from hatred, or hurls something at another, lying in wait, and death ensues, 21 or in enmity strikes another with the hand, and death ensues, then the one who struck the blow shall be put to death; that person is a murderer; the avenger of blood shall put the murderer to death, when they meet.

But if the slayer shall at any time go outside the bounds of the original city of refuge, . . . and is killed by the avenger, no bloodguilt shall be incurred. —
Numbers 35:26-27

These are fairly standard indications that a person acted intentionally. We can agree generally with the justice for which this system is designed, though most of us would regard it as horribly unfair were it to apply to us. Supposing that if you killed someone in a car accident, would you regard it as fair if your only recourse was to flee to a specific place of refuge, while if a relative of the person you killed caught you, they could kill you.

22 But if someone pushes another suddenly without enmity, or hurls any object without lying in wait, 23 or, while handling any stone that could cause death, *unintentionally drops it on another and death ensues, though they were not enemies, and no harm was intended, ²⁴ then the congregation shall judge between the slayer and the avenger of blood, in accordance with these ordinances; ²⁵ and the congregation shall rescue the slayer from the avenger of blood. Then the congregation shall send the slayer back to the original city of refuge. The slayer shall live in it until the death of the high priest who was anointed with the holy oil.*

²⁶ But if the slayer shall at any time go outside the bounds of the original city of refuge, ²⁷ and is found by the avenger of blood outside the bounds of the city of refuge, and is killed by the avenger, <u>no bloodguilt shall be incurred.</u> ²⁸ For the slayer must remain in the city of refuge until the death of the high priest; but after the death of the high priest the slayer may return home.

Now you add the additional unfairness, from our point of view, of the person who has simply had an accident having to live in the city of refuge for what appears to us to be an arbitrary length of time.

The cities of refuge don't present an ideal.

²⁹ These things shall be a statute and ordinance for you throughout your generations wherever you live. — Numbers 35:9-29 (NRSV)

You can extrapolate the existing situation from the statements in the chapter itself. If one Israelite killed another, a relative of the slain might could seek vengeance, irrespective of whether the person did so intentionally or not. So God introduced the cities of refuge. Now note here that we are not looking at some of the better laws, even of the Torah itself that tell the people not to harm a neighbor. The law provides a place of refuge so that an innocent person can flee there and be safe from the avenger. A trial can be held, and if the person is found to have killed intentionally, then he is no longer safe. In addition, he must spend the remainder of the life of the High Priest in the city of refuge.

Now this law leaves a number of weaknesses:

1. If the avenger can get the killer before he makes it to the city, he can kill him.
2. The killer must stay in the city for what might be a very long period of time.
3. The execution of justice is still left to one seeking vengeance as a general rule.

The cities of refuge in Numbers 35 thus don't present an ideal. What they do is show God providing a limiting rule on an existing custom of vengeance to make it more humane. Romans 12:19 presents an even more humane solution as does Leviticus 19:18. But God knew that an ingrained command could not be dealt with simply by saying it was to go away. Thus he also established limits on the practice of vengeance, leading the way toward a better world of forgiveness, and of justice executed by more impartial persons.

MESSENGERS – GOD AND PROPHET

THE NATURE OF PROPHECY

Most prophecy was originally expressed orally. The prophet went to the person or persons to whom the message applied and spoke that message to them. Thus at its foundation, prophecy is speaking the word or message that God has for a particular circumstance or time. In Biblical times prophets foretold the future, condemned unrighteous acts, gave encouragement, recommended courses of action to rulers or to priests and warned of judgment. Only a small portion of the work of a prophet involves predicting the future, and even the predictions are designed either to teach or to correct.

Only a small portion of the work of a prophet involves predicting the future.

There is a variant on this in the knew testament, called the gift of prophecy. A person who has the gift of prophecy is a member of the congregation who receives messages from the Lord to speak forth. These messages can come at any time or place and are often not under the conscious control of the person who speaks them so that the person speaking does not choose whether to utter the message. (If the gift of prophecy is true, the message will always be from God, of course.)

Unlike many of the Old Testament prophets, the person with the gift of prophecy is generally a part of the structure of the church, rather than someone who stands outside it. This is consistent with the gift of the Holy Spirit to the church at Pentecost. Rather than being a gift for a special few, God's Spirit is poured out on everybody, though God gives different gifts. The body as a whole is supposed to act together. So the person exercising the office of prophet within the church has a different role than the individual prophet of Old Testament times.

The true prophet is one who is not part of the structure and who does not work as a team with the king. His job is to challenge the king.

To see the difference between the two roles, compare the story of Micaiah in 1 Kings 22 with 1 Corinthians 14:29-32. (I discuss this chapter in more detail on page 72.) While there are prophets that the king gathers to give him words he wants to hear, the true prophet is one who is not part of the structure and who does not work as a team with the king. His job is to challenge the king. This role is even more forcefully displayed by Elijah in 1 Kings 17, when he confronts the king and tells him there will be no rain for a few years until he, Elijah, says so.

By contrast in 1 Corinthians the speaking of the prophets is a controlled part of the worship service, the contribution of the prophets to the faith community. Their gifts are among those gifts given within the church according to the decision of the Holy Spirit. The office of prophet similarly places the prophet within the structure of the church, rather than as an outsider who challenges the decisions of church and state.

The office of the prophet is one established in the church to provide continuing correction and guidance from a person that the church recognizes as possessing a true gift. The church also recognizes that the person is reliable in the exercise of that gift and has the wisdom to use it properly. In appointing someone to the office of prophet, the church recognizes that the person so commissioned will speak the word of the Lord only when he or she is certain that a message is from God.

Pastors, evangelists, teachers and other church leaders, as well as those exercising the office of the prophet must apply discernment to any message identified as a word from the Lord, and must correct those who express a false word.

The gift of prophecy is one of the information types of gifts given by the Holy Spirit. Others are words of knowledge or wisdom and discernment. Prophecy is distinguished from these other gifts in that it provides a direct message from God and is usually identified as the word of the Lord when the prophet speaks it in one way or another, though not always.

Don't let the speaker, writer or the form in which the message comes distract you from the message.

A person with the gift of prophecy may receive messages in various ways, including visions (Ezekiel 1), dreams (Daniel 7), words of knowledge or wisdom, discernment and the operation of another spiritual gift such as teaching (Paul's epistles, Hebrews, James). Very often the prophet's message will come in a way that requires the prophet to find the words to describe the message. It may even be in the form of a strong emotional impression.

A prophecy may be expressed in words appropriate to the personality of the person expressing the message, and to the audience that is to receive it. Often people exercising the prophetic gift try to use theological wording, Biblical phrases or even archaic language to express the prophecy. It is alright, however, to express a message you have received from God in ordinary speech. That is one the ancient prophets did.

In receiving the Word of the Lord, we must separate the way the message is delivered from the message itself. God has always used a variety of messengers and methods to present His word. Don't let the speaker, writer or the form in which the message comes distract you from the message.

Both the message of someone exercising the gift of prophecy and the Bible can bring us God's message. In the case of the Bible, however, we have a message that has stood the test of years of use and acceptance of the church, guided by the Holy Spirit.

The Word as revealed in scripture is thus the standard by which other words are judged.

The Word as revealed in scripture is thus the standard by which other words are judged. Unlike Abraham, we have the benefit of both the scriptures and the tradition of the church by which to judge our own individual experiences.

The penalty for false prophecy in Biblical times was death (Deuteronomy 18:20). While we don't have the death penalty in church life today, one should always be careful when claiming that something is a word from the Lord. God's name is not to be taken carelessly or lightly. So pastors and other leaders must use discernment in dealing with those who claim a word from the Lord.

THE SOURCE OF AUTHORITY

In the modern church we place a great deal of importance on succession. Who laid hands on any particular person to pass on his authority? There is the cute rhyme written by Charles Wesley regarding John Wesley's ordination of Thomas Coke for his American mission. Wesley, not being a Bishop, was not authorized to ordain anyone:

So easily are Bishops made,
By man or woman's whim?
Wesley his hands on Coke hath laid,
But who laid hands on him?[7]

Charles Wesley's concern sounds a little quaint to modern Methodists, but it was and is a very real concern for many Christians. The question gets asked less frequently in Methodism because there is now a *Methodist* tradition, but if an individual Methodist pastor established a new church, someone would be bound to ask who laid hands on *him*.

There is a certain amount of scriptural support for this position in the Old Testament with the story of Elijah and Elisha. Elisha sticks with Elijah in order to receive his power when he leaves (2 Kings 2:1-18). A large amount of vocabulary in the modern church comes from this particular story.

> *"But the LORD took me from tending the flock and said to me, 'Go, prophesy to my people Israel.'"* — *Amos 7:15 (TNIV)*

But when we base most of our ideas about God's call and anointing on this passage we are ignoring the broader sweep of history where, at a minimum, any human source of a prophet's power is ignored. While there are schools of the prophets, we rarely hear of a new graduate of one of those schools going out with his diploma and beginning to prophesy.

There are, indeed cases in which such background is outright denied. Amos provides such a denial after he was ordered to quit prophesying in Bethel.

> *Amos answered Amaziah, "I was neither a prophet nor the disciple of a prophet, but I was a shepherd, and I*

---

7 Quoted from Jennifer Woodruff Tait, "Charles Wesley: Family Man of Methodism," <u>Circuit Rider</u> September/October 2006, p. 6, last accessed 4/11/07.

also took care of sycamore-fig trees. But the LORD took me from tending the flock and said to me, 'Go, prophesy to my people Israel.'" — *Amos 7:14-15 (TNIV)*

Amos knows that the one thing he needs is the call of the Lord and that the opposition to his message comes not from a problem with his spiritual pedigree, but with a rejection of the message that he is presenting.

Paul, in writing to the Galatians, takes pains to make it clear that he did not receive his message from anyone, and that nothing has been added to it by anyone else. His message is strictly the revelation of God, and God's call working through him.

Rather than trying to establish his authority through ties to the recognized apostles, Paul makes every effort to distinguish himself from them.

He introduces himself—or reintroduces himself—to the Galatian churches as "an apostle—sent not with a human commission nor by human authority, but by Jesus Christ and God the Father who raised him from the dead" (Galatians 1:1 TNIV). He continues this argument with his account of the Jerusalem conference. Rather than saying that he convinced the Jerusalem leaders, or that they had come to a compromise, he notes that they "added nothing to his message" and then announces:

On the contrary, they saw that I had been entrusted with the task of preaching the gospel to the Gentiles, just as Peter had been to the Jews. For God, who was at work in Peter as an apostle to the Jews was also at work in me as an apostle to the Gentiles. — Galatians 2:7-8 (TNIV)

Paul is at great pains to do just the opposite of what we expect someone to do today.[8] Rather than trying to establish his authority through ties to the recognized apostles, he makes every effort to distinguish himself from them. To him it is clear that God is working through him, no matter what men may have said. And even though it is reported in Acts that Paul and Barnabas were sent out by laying on of hands in the Antioch church, Paul never mentions that commission.

Someone is sure to object that Paul was an apostle, and thus the rules are different. He's speaking authoritatively by inspiration of God. But that is precisely the point that is not determined at this point in the story. People are questioning whether Paul is, in fact, speaking for God, and whether he has the authority to do what he is doing.

He could certainly make a claim that he had been commissioned at that conference, but to him it is more important to make the clear claim that God is working in his life, that he is called and commissioned by God, and that God is the source of his authority.

> *To Paul it is more important to make the clear claim that God is working in his life, that he is called and commissioned by God, and that God is the source of his authority.*

Too frequently we forget just what the historical situation was when we provide a doctrinal interpretation for such a passage of scripture. It's easy for us to read Paul's apostleship and recognized authority as a writer of scripture into the passage. But at this point while Paul was recognized as an apostle by some, there were others who were questioning that authority and the authenticity of his mission.

We cannot assume the conclusion by letting Paul's authority settle an argument that would never occur had it actually been settled at that point.

---

8 I am indebted in my understanding of this passage to J. Louis Martyn, Galatians (Anchor Bible), New York: Doubleday, 1997.

Hearing – Message and Community

The focus of many discussions of inspiration is entirely centered on the way that God communicates the message to the prophet, with the vision sometimes extended to include how that message gets written down. When we look at revelation as a complete process of communication we will be equally interested in how people receive the message.

> *When we look at revelation as a complete process of communication we will be equally interested in how people receive the message.*

Information or Conversation

Discussions that are centered on God and the message frequently center around such texts as 2 Timothy 3:16, 2 Peter 1:20-21, or Hebrews 4:12. Now all of these are good texts from which to study about the nature of scripture, but it interests me that we build theology from these texts which we then try to impose on the remainder of scripture, rarely bothering to spend time observing just how the process of revelation has functioned.

My idea here is not to find a different set of texts from which to extract theological propositions, but rather to look at the narrative, and ask how God has managed to reveal himself at various times and under various circumstances. By observing the narrative of scripture, we can get a better idea of what the propositions of scripture mean in practice. When 2 Timothy 3:16 says that scripture is profitable for certain things, we can ask precisely how scripture was used in accomplishing such things.

Our focus will be on the **story** rather than on the **commentary**, or one might say the experience rather than the propositions. This is not because the scripture does not contain propositional truth. I believe one can derive propositional truths from the *Focus on the story* story and from the explicit statements, but if *rather than on the* we read these always in the context of the *commentary, on* story, we will get more accurate propositions *the experience* that are also more easily understood. After all, *rather than the* there must be some reason why God put so *propositions.* much story in scripture, and why even all those propositions arrived in the framework of the story.

In a discussion some time ago, I annoyed someone when I made my normal suggestion to look at places other than these standard texts in discussing inspiration. In particular, I was recommending the story of Jeremiah and Baruch as they produced the scroll of Jeremiah's prophecies (Jeremiah 36), to help us understand just how inspiration works. Now we're going to discuss the standard texts a number of times in this book, but let's look at the story first.

What can we learn from this story?

- ✔ The prophecy itself may occur at some time earlier than the writing.
- ✔ It may not be the prophet's own pen that does the writing.
- ✔ The writings of a prophet may be written at more than one time; this may point us toward an explanation for why we

have multiple versions of the book of Jeremiah with material in a different order.

- ✔ The prophecy in both spoken and written form is produced in response to a need.
- ✔ God's word sometimes comes at a considerable cost to the messenger.

Those are just a few things. As we read the story of Jeremiah we can learn not only about God's method of revelation but how God's inspiration works with the inspired person. This is one of the things I mean by participatory Bible study. "Participatory" can mean simply to participate in the process of study–everyone in a group reads a text, makes a comment, looks something up in a reference source, etc. But what I mean is investing oneself in the actual story of the scriptures, participating in it through the imagination, and then viewing one's present life as a continuation of that story of God's action in history. My question here is not just how Jeremiah heard from God, and what Jeremiah had to say, but how can I hear from God, and from there how I can build a relationship with God, and how Jeremiah's experience can help me with mine.

There must be some reason why God put so much story in scripture!

We go to the Bible looking for information; God goes to the Bible looking for conversation.

God doesn't merely want to *inform* you. That could be done much more easily than the process that brought us the Bible. God wants to relate to you, have a conversation with you.

And if you can see that in Jeremiah, it's going to help. The agony of his situation as people ignore his message. His horror as his nation continues to follow the path of destruction. His frustration as people won't listen to his message. Then we get the command to produce this scroll. We see it destroyed and replaced. Live this with Jeremiah! How much is this like our Christian experience as God tries to get through to us, to get us to listen, to get us to persevere in his word?

A Tale of Three Prophets

One element of God's method of revealing himself to people is that he chooses specific people to accomplish specific missions. These people are often a particular fit for a particular situation.

I want to look at the time of the exile, and three of God's messengers, Jeremiah, Daniel, and Ezekiel. Now there will be those who accept a later date for Daniel and will question my using him in this part of the story. Let me simply state that I do believe that the stories of Daniel, though perhaps not the entire book, date from the time of the exile, were later written down and collected in what we now have as the Aramaic portions of Daniel. So for purposes of this discussion, I will treat Daniel as a historical person who had a prophetic ministry in the court of Babylon at the time of the exile. If he didn't exist, we would have to invent him!

Specific people are chosen for specific missions.

At the time of the exile there were three distinct situations, three distinct groups of people to whom God needed to communicate his message. The first was the people of Judah who were rapidly heading toward exile and destruction. The second group was those who were already exiled and living in Babylon. The third was the Babylonian court, both the Babylonian king and officials for whom God had a mission, but also the exiles who were living in a state of privilege at the court and facing the temptation to compromise away their faith.

The inhabitants of Judah were living in a dreamworld of security, based on the belief that the presence of the temple, and thus God's presence, protected Jerusalem no matter what. The exiles in Babylon generally felt abandoned by God and either waited expectantly for their soon return or began to simply give up. At the same time the king of Babylon took the view that he was favored of the gods because of his successes, and those who lived in his court faced the constant danger of compromise of their principles in order to gain power and favor and even permanence in their new situation. Any of these attitudes presented a barrier to God's plan.

God's response was not merely to present the facts. The facts were that the exile would be long but temporary, and that in the end the people would return. Jerusalem would be destroyed, but it would be rebuilt. Nebuchadnezzar was a great king and conqueror, but he also was limited and temporary and the way to success for the Jewish young people who found themselves there was faithfulness, not compromise. Even if they suffered for their faithfulness, the consequences of compromise would be even deeper.

Those were the facts, but God still needed messengers. None of the audiences actually wanted to listen, but there were ways to make things clear, and to get at least some of them to listen.

For Judah, there was Jeremiah, the weeping prophet. Not only one who could speak the message, but one who could *weep* the message, whose very life symbolized God's love for Judah and his unwillingness to give up his people. God's sorrow was expressed in the form of a prophet who spoke, suffered, cried, and was ignored, but who never gave up, who kept speaking until there was nothing left.

None of the audiences actually wanted to listen.

Ezekiel was himself an exile, capable of understanding the situation of other exiles. His inaugural vision (Ezekiel 1) reassured Ezekiel that God was still with the exiles, that in spite of judgment there was hope. Yahweh was not a territorial god, incapable of caring for his people outside of their own land. The message became a part of Ezekiel. But the presentation was different from that of Jeremiah. Ezekiel was not allowed to mourn his own wife's death (Ezekiel 24:15-27). Both his visions and his methods of expression were powerful and creative.

Daniel was one tempted to compromise in the court of the king. He had every opportunity to go over to the side of the winner, and to accept Nebuchadnezzar as the once and always king of the world. But he stood quietly for God and for faithfulness to his message.

Three messengers with similar messages, but different audiences, and different means to present that message—God involved in the daily activities of human beings, a microcosm of God acting in the flesh.

IMPORTANT STORIES OF HEARING

MICAIAH (1 KINGS 22:1-38)

Micaiah was a true prophet, who ministered in Israel during the time of Ahab, but he was surrounded by quite a number of false prophets. Some of these were actually probably worshipers of Baal, but others were simply willing to sell the "word of the Lord" either for money or for fame.

Ahab produces four hundred prophets, all of whom assure him that Yahweh is with him.

We encounter Micaiah when Jehoshaphat, King of Judah is visiting Ahab, King of Israel, and they want to go and retake Ramoth in Gilead, which was occupied by the Syrians. It is clear from the congregation that both kings are very anxious to go to battle, but Jehoshaphat, a godly king, wanted to hear from a prophet first (v. 5).

Ahab can do better than that. He produces four hundred prophets, all of whom assure him that Yahweh is with him, and that he will win.

We are not told what tips Jehoshaphat off to the problem. It could be that he had a hard time imagining God being that favorable to his northern colleague, whose character was not the best. Whether this was Jehoshaphat's thinking or not, it is valid. If you hear someone prophesying favorably about someone who is not right with God, you should consider things carefully. There may be some false prophecy going on (cf. Deuteronomy 13:1-5).

Jehoshaphat could well have been concerned about the need for 400 prophets and their unanimity. We don't know how prophecy was handled in Judah, but we do not have any stories of large groups of prophets as we do in the north. All of the cases of large crowds of people prophesying are stories of false prophets.

Whatever tipped him off, Jehoshaphat wants to hear from another prophet. Consider the way in which Ahab, the man in power, regards Micaiah, the true prophet of Yahweh:

> **8** *"We could ask Micaiah son of Imlah," Ahab said. "But I hate Micaiah. He always has bad news for me."*
> — *1 Kings 22:8*

A true prophet of Yahweh often stands alone, and is often not well liked by the people in temporal authority. The 400 prophets are seeking fame and the gratitude of their monarch. If the king wins, they will likely be rewarded for their prophetic "advice." If the king loses, perhaps he'll be dead, and they can start working on the next king. The prophetic office is a lonely job, because so frequently the task of the prophet is to rebuke.

A true prophet of Yahweh often stands alone, and is often not well liked by the people in temporal authority.

When Micaiah comes out he tries to go along with the crowd, but both Ahab and Jehoshaphat know that he is not telling the truth. When Ahab commands him to tell the truth, he says:

> **17** *He answered, "In a vision I saw Israelite soldiers walking around in the hills like sheep without a shepherd to guide them. The LORD said, 'This army has no leader. They should go home and not fight.' "*

> **18** *Ahab turned to Jehoshaphat and said, "I told you he would bring bad news!"*

19 *Micaiah replied:*

Listen to this! I also saw the L*ORD* *seated on his throne with every creature in heaven gathered around him.* *20* *The* L*ORD* *asked, "Who can trick Ahab and make him go to Ramoth where he will be killed?"*

They talked about it for a while, *21* *then finally a spirit came forward and said to the* L*ORD*, *"I can trick Ahab."*

"How?" the L*ORD* *asked.*

22 *"I'll make Ahab's prophets lie to him."*

"Good!" the L*ORD* *replied. "Now go and do it."*

23 *This is exactly what has happened, Ahab. The* L*ORD* *made all your prophets lie to you, and he knows you will soon be destroyed.*

24 *Zedekiah walked up to Micaiah and slapped him on the face. Then he asked, "Do you really think the* L*ORD* *would speak to you and not to me?"*

25 *Micaiah answered, "You'll find out on the day you have to hide in the back room of some house."*

26 *Ahab shouted, "Arrest Micaiah! Take him to Prince Joash and Governor Amon of Samaria.* *27* *Tell them to put him in prison and to give him nothing but bread and water until I come back safely."*

^{28} *Micaiah said, "If you do come back, I was wrong about what the LORD wanted me to say." Then he told the crowd, "Don't forget what I said!" — 1 Kings 22:17-28 (CEV)*

In the end the Israelites lose, Ahab is killed and Micaiah is vindicated. But at this point in the story Micaiah has to stand firm and alone in presenting the word that God has given him to present.

Is it really possible for the Lord to deceive someone the way Micaiah's vision presents it? Many people ignore a story such as this in favor of believing that God cannot lie (Titus 1:2). Now I believe that God allowed the people here to believe that he was the one who inspired the lie because he was not yet ready to talk to them about Satan and his deceptive works.[9] But even if deceptive activities are assigned to Satan, God still permits someone to present a deceptive word to the leaders here. The leaders are expected to discern.

In this case, the result of wrong discernment is death.

In Ahab's case, the result of wrong discernment was death.

JEREMIAH AND THE JUDEAN REMNANT (JEREMIAH 42:1-43:13)

This is a fascinating story and is so typical of the common response to prophets. The scripture is much too long to quote, but the story goes like this.

The Jews who remained in Judea are afraid of Babylonian retaliation because one of them had killed Gedaliah, the governor appointed by the king of Babylon. They are not being paranoid; it was very likely

---

9 For more on this see Thompson, Alden, Who's Afraid of the Old Testament God? Gonzalez, FL: Energion Publications, 2003, chapter 3,"Whatever happened to Satan in the Old Testament?' pp. 33-53.

that the king of Babylon would be extremely angry over the murder of his governor.

So all the people gather together to ask Jeremiah for a word from the Lord. They want to know what they should do (42:1-4). They claim that they will obey whatever the Lord tells Jeremiah, whether it is favorable or unfavorable.

So often when we look for a word from the Lord we already know what we want the word to be. In spite of their promise, these men have a very specific plan. They hope that Jeremiah will tell them that God has commanded them to do precisely what they want to do anyhow.

Often when we look for a word from the Lord we already know what we want the word to be. Jeremiah receives a word from the Lord ten days later. In summary, they are told to stay where they are and warned against going to Egypt (42:7-22). By the way the the message from God is worded, it is clear that the people have in mind going to Egypt. I suspect that Jeremiah was unaware of this, and thus took seriously the promise of the leaders that they would obey whatever word he got.

As soon as Jeremiah is done giving them the word of the Lord, the leaders change their mind. They had hoped to have God's command to do what they wanted to do anyhow, but once God's word went against them, they had to play it down. The accuse Baruch of inciting Jeremiah to go against them, and accuse Jeremiah of lying. Then they promptly go to Egypt as they had planned to all along.

Part of listening to God, and of course of obedience to God, is being willing to surrender our agendas when God commands otherwise. If we are not willing to surrender those agendas, we might as well not ask God for guidance.

BALAAM (NUMBERS 22-24)

In Numbers 22-24 we find the story of Balaam, a prophet of Yahweh whose origins are mysterious. Balak, King of Moab, wanted Balaam for a simple job, or at least Balak thought the job would be simple. To him it seemed quite appropriate that a soothsayer should be able to slant the message the right way.

In Balaam's case, however, this was not so, because Balaam was a prophet of Yahweh, and Yahweh controls his own word. Thus through multiple tries, Balaam is unable to provide the curse.

It's interesting that he tries, because he indicates to Balak from the start that he will be unable to say whatever Yahweh gives him to say. Both men seem optimistic.

The view in ancient paganism was that the gods could and should be manipulated. That was the purpose of sacrifices and offerings. But God does not work that way. Those who try to manipulate God generally find themselves in serious trouble.

Those who try to manipulate God generally find themselves in serious trouble.

In the case of Balaam, however, determination to bring a curse on Israel brought him to a point of scheming, so that eventually he joins in a scheme to lead Israel into sin and thus bring a curse on themselves (Numbers 25, 2 Peter 2:15). For this he eventually died (Numbers 31:8).

HEARING GOD PERSONALLY

While I will discuss some barriers to hearing God's word in the next chapter, I want to present a few ideas about how we personally hear —or fail to hear—the message that God has for us.[10]

---

10 This section comes from a series of devotionals I wrote for my wife Jody's devotional list, http://jody.energion.com.

*(1) YHWH said to Abram, Leave your homeland, your
relatives, and your father's household and go to a land
that I will show you. (2) And I will make you a great
nation, and I will bless you and make your reputation
great, and you will be a blessing. (3) And I will bless
those who bless you and curse those who curse you,
and all the peoples of the earth will be blessed through
you. (4) And Abram went as YHWH had commanded
him, and Lot went with him. — Genesis 12:1-4a (HN)*

Have you ever really thought about this verse? I know I was well into
my experience as a Bible teacher before I did. Earlier we talked about
Abraham and the command God gave to him. Can we really follow
God in the way that Abraham did, even considering that we have
more so much more to work with than he did?

*Abraham
didn't have
the benefit of
the Bible
against which
to compare
what he
heard.*

That's a pretty good question for me. Even after I
have written about Abraham and his obedience, I
have to ask myself: Have I really heard those
questions?

You see, Abraham didn't have the benefit of the
Bible against which to compare what he heard.
According to Joshua 24:2, he was worshiping other
Gods at this time. He had next to nothing to go on
so as to be sure he was hearing what God said, yet somehow he
became convinced he was hearing from God and that he should
obey. No wonder his faith was counted as righteousness (Genesis
15:6)!

How do I match up? Well, I dither about whether God is really
speaking, and then I wonder about the timing, the finances, what the
neighbors will think, what my family will think, and on and on. By
the time I get around to doing, it can easily be too late.

Now I'm not suggesting that God's normal way of doing things is to
order people to move without a plan. Lots of people have thought

they had such an order from God and they disrupted their families and their own lives, and eventually found themselves in serious trouble. That's why the Bible also calls for wisdom. Right after you think God is telling you something, it's a great idea to claim the promise of James 1:5 and ask for wisdom!

But what I do ask you to think about today is this: Is God willing to talk to you today, as you work, play, think, and talk? Are you willing to listen and obey when you do know that it is God speaking?

We're often afraid to admit we hear God speak, because it sounds a bit like insanity. But if it is insanity, then it's a form of insanity that has been common to people of faith at least since Abraham. Perhaps it's time to get comfortable with it.

God is speaking. Are you listening? If not, perhaps you have a problem with the messenger.

We're often afraid to admit we hear God speak, because it sounds a bit like insanity.

¹He went out from there and came to his home country, and his disciples followed him. ²And when it was Sabbath, he began to preach in the synagogue, and many were amazed when they heard him. They said, "Where did this guy get these things, and what is this wisdom that has been given to him, and the these miracles that happen through his hands? ³Is this not the carpenter, the son of Mary and the brother of James and Justus and Jude and Simon? Are not his sisters here with us? And they were offended by him. ⁴And Jesus said to them, "A prophet is not without honor except in his own country and among his relatives and in his household." ⁵And he wasn't able to perform any miracles except to place his hands on a few sick people and heal them. ⁶And he was amazed because of their unbelief. Then he traveled in the surrounding villages teaching. — Mark 6:1-6 (HN)

We normally teach and preach this passage from the point of view of the prophet. Poor prophet! Can't get heard in his own country. And it's true that it's very difficult for anyone with any expertise to get heard by people who know him well. The people who remember you when you were in the church nursery in diapers have a hard time respecting you as an expert, particularly in spiritual matters. The bigger the claims, in that case, the less likely they are to be accepted. Or so it seems.

But what about the other side, the family, friends, and neighbors who refuse to listen? Earlier I wrote about listening to God, and asked whether we were ready to listen to God as Abraham did. I asked if we would be willing to do what Abraham did and move out of our homes without knowing where we're going, just because God has spoken.

The people who remember you when you were in the church nursery in diapers have a hard time respecting you as an expert.

Even though that sort of idea tends to scare us, and sounds somewhat like insanity, there's a certain dignity to it. "I heard God's voice," someone says, "And I'm doing just what he said." It sounds so pious and close to God.

But supposing God wants to speak to you through that child you cared for in the nursery? What's going to happen then? Will you say, "I knew you when you were in diapers," and miss the message God has for you? What if God wants to speak to you through a teenager in your church? Will you be so busy remembering all the annoying teen behavior that you can't hear the message God has for you? What if the messenger is a homeless person who has come to you for help? Will the economic status of the messenger shut your ears?

I think this is critical, because in my experience God is much more likely to tell us something through a person we're involved with in daily life than he is to speak with a voice from heaven. I'm not talking about the person who puts on a solemn "prophet face" and announces "thus saith the Lord," followed by a supposedly divine message. Rather, I'm thinking of the person who says something to you and you suddenly know that you really needed to hear that.

Sometimes we're eagerly waiting for a voice from God, or someone to show up with the proper credentials, such as degrees or the endorsement of anointed leaders, when God has been speaking to us through the normal, subtle channels he prefers, and we just haven't been listening. Remember that the most thunderous messages of the prophets were reserved not for the especially deserving, but rather for the stubbornly unhearing and disobedient. Elijah was not sent to the 7,000 faithful in Israel (1 Kings 19:18), but to Ahab, who rejected God's voice to the last.

What does God have to do to get your attention?

> *Elijah was not sent to the 7,000 faithful in Israel but to Ahab, who rejected God's voice to the last.*

¹⁷For Herod had sent and seized John and bound him in prison because of Herodias, his brother Philip's wife, whom he had married. ¹⁸Because John told Herod that it was wrong to take his brother's wife. ¹⁹And Herodias hated him, and wanted to kill him, but she couldn't. ²⁰For Herod was afraid of John, because he knew that he was a righteous and holy man. But he kept John locked up, and listened to him, even though he was deeply troubled by what John said. — Mark 6:17-20 (HN)

This text provides an example of listening, but not doing anything about what God has said.

People who have come to me for prayer or have Bible questions very often are looking for guidance from God. They want God to tell them what to do. But I've noticed that while some genuinely don't know what the right thing to do is, with a little discussion and thinking, most actually do know, but they're hoping to hear something else. I remember once myself that I was diligently seeking guidance from the Lord. I knew I hadn't heard anything, not so much as a vague impression. Then suddenly one morning in my time of prayer it hit me. There was a right thing to do and a wrong thing, and I needed no other guidance. I simply hadn't looked at the problem from the proper angle to see that one of the options I was considering was wrong.

Herod is in a situation that is troubling to him. He's done something wrong and John the Baptist has called him on it. As a powerful ruler, Herod didn't have to put up with such things. He could call for the accuser's head and thus deal with the accusation. But Herod does what we often do. He sets it aside and doesn't take action. Herodias wants John dead, but Herod won't do it. Why?

By keeping the messenger locked up he keeps the message locked up, and he doesn't have to act.

I think it's clear that Herod knows that John the Baptist is right. He knows that John is a godly man. So he compromises. He doesn't act on what John has said to him, but he also doesn't execute him. He goes and listens to him, even though he's troubled by what he hears. By keeping the messenger locked up he keeps the message locked up, and he doesn't have to act. So he toy's with God's messenger and God's message.

Now there's such a thing as (patiently?) waiting on God's timing, but there's also procrastinating when you know what is right. While you procrastinate, you may be thinking that you haven't rejected God's message. No, you've just set it aside to think about. You'll do the right thing, but you'll do it later.

Beware of Herod's trap. Somewhere, sometime, you are going to act on the message. You may just let it slide into oblivion, or you may be trapped, like Herod, into forcefully rejecting both message and messenger. God's word doesn't go back to him empty, but accomplishes what he sent it to do (Isaiah 55:11). That doesn't mean that you get the blessing, however. God's word may accomplish its mission through somebody else.

Do you have any of God's messages or messengers held in prison? No, I know you don't have a jail to lock them up physically. But are you procrastinating about things that you know are right? Let the word out of prison before you are manipulated into carrying out an execution!

PRACTICAL CONSIDERATIONS OF HEARING

Imagine a church committee meeting where a number of leaders in a particular area of ministry. Someone speaks earnestly to the group. It might be the pastor or the chairperson. It might just be an individual of influence.

"I have been praying about this for weeks," he or she says, "and this morning God spoke to me during my devotions. He told me that we should undertake this project. It's God's will. I know it looks like there is no money, and there are not enough volunteers, but God says that if we do this, the money and the people will come."

There is a constant temptation in church discussions to bring God into the situation.

Silence follows. Members who have been objecting squirm in their seats and wonder what to say. Should they just capitulate? After all, who can argue against God?

For many, especially in charismatic or pentecostal churches, this will be a familiar situation, but it is not restricted to those churches. There is a constant temptation in church discussions to bring God into the situation. We are, after all, praying for God's guidance. Shouldn't we be happy to discover that God has, in fact, spoken, and that he has chosen a member of our little committee in our one congregation through which to give his word? Should we not simply accept the word that is given? We prayed for it, after all!

If you read this far, and didn't just skip to this chapter, you will realize that I do believe that God can speak at any time and to any person. He is not restricted to the pages of the Bible, nor to ordained clergy, bishops, special intercessors, or any particular category of people.

But it is crucial to notice that we do not have any guarantee that God has spoken in this particular committee meeting. We may know and trust the person who is making the claim, but God's command is to test everything, and that includes a statement by our pastor that God has spoken to him in his morning devotions.

God's command is to test everything.

19 Don't turn away God's Spirit 20 or ignore prophecies. 21 Put everything to the test. Accept what is good 22 and don't have anything to do with evil. —
1 Thessalonians 5:19-22 (CEV)

Note the four elements that are required by this scripture:

1. Listen – do not ignore (v. 20)
2. Test – do not simply accept the claim, nor reject it because you're sure God can't speak that way (v. 21a)
3. Accept what is good (v 21b)
4. Keep away from what is evil (v. 22)

Now you may object that the person who spoke in the committee didn't claim to be a prophet, and that is true. But he did claim that what he was saying constituted God's guidance for the situation. I believe it is critical that we recognize that as soon as someone claims to speak for God in any way, testing becomes imperative. This applies in the church as well as in our personal decision making. Too often we let the *claim* that God has spoken end the discussion, when the discussion should only be ended by the *conclusion* that God has spoken.

When we test, we also put ourselves in the position of the person who spoke God's word; if we say it is not God's word, we are taking a similar level of spiritual risk, and we must be prepared to stand for what we say.

Frequently, church leaders avoid this whole problem. When people make a claim to speak for God they are either received as prophets, and their words accepted as God's words, or they are put into a sort of limbo category, where they are generally ignored. But to do that is to avoid the responsibility God has laid on church leaders to test.

Testing the Claim

Church leaders have the responsibility to test claims to speak for God in the church.

I will discuss how one tests such things in more detail later, but there are some key things to look at immediately. It is quite possible for a sincere person to use the claim that God has spoken manipulatively. One warning sign is when someone has argued for a particular course of action and consistently been losing the argument, and then suddenly receives a word from God that they were absolutely right all along, and that the only way the church can receive a blessing is if they will do as that person desires.

But there are some other warning signs:

✔ The proposed course of action violates ethical or moral standards.
  You might be amazed at how frequently this occurs, and how easy it is to rationalize immoral behavior when someone is forcefully claiming that God has ordered it. Some people have claimed that God sanctioned adultery for them on some basis. I know of cases in which someone decided that God

had ordered them to spend their rent money on a mission trip, and not pay their rent. If done without the permission of their landlord, that is at least unethical, and should cause one to consider carefully whether God is speaking. Don't be led into immoral or unethical actions by a voice.

✔ "God's words" come to a person in the course of debate. God's command should generally be complete and straightforward, and shouldn't require amendment. If "God" keeps coming up with new arguments over the course of the debate, just as an ordinary person would, think again.

✔ "God's words" are presented in a divisive way, or introduce an element of divisiveness.

"Words from the Lord" that involve gossip, criticism, a judgmental spirit, or cruelty should be rejected.

Make no mistake, God's words through prophets do produce negative reactions in those who do not want to obey God. Where divisiveness comes into the discussion is something that also requires discernment and testing. We would not want to reject God's word on the basis that it made the devil angry! "Words from the Lord" that involve gossip, criticism, a judgmental spirit, or cruelty should be rejected.

✔ The person who presents God's word reacts angrily to having that word tested by others.
When someone is sure that God has spoken and others reject that word, it is appropriate for them to be grieved at that event, but they should welcome discernment and sincere testing, and they should be prepared to live with differences of opinion.

✔ "God's words" deny established scriptural standards. Continuing revelation should not reverse what God has already said. The Bible has been tested and accepted by the church, so if you reverse major principles of scriptures, you are likely off track. This doesn't mean that interpretations cannot be corrected, but soundly interpreted scripture should be upheld.

How does one respond to a claim to speak for God? It depends on the particular circumstances. If you are in a church where testing is regularly practiced, you already have a path to follow. Hopefully this will end either with acceptance of the word, or a gracious—and I emphasize gracious—rejection with explanation and correction provided to the person who made the claim in the first place. If you cannot graciously respond, even when you reject the word, you likely need to examine yourself.

Outside of that atmosphere, when I am not sure that what someone has claimed as a word from God actually is such a word, I will often choose to say simply, "God is going to have to tell me that," or "That is not what I hear." If you are not in a congregational setting where there is a commonality of beliefs, responding appropriately to a false word is not so easy.

It is not my responsibility or even my right to correct everyone in sight.

If I am visiting a congregation, it is not my responsibility or even my right to correct everyone in sight. The idea of God speaking requires that we work in community, with a common set of principles to apply before we can correct one another. Even when I am teaching in a church that is not my home church, if I hear something said as a word from God—and I have heard such!—I will tell the pastor. I do not correct someone in his congregation myself unless he specifically asks me to.

The full process of testing that ends with either acceptance or appropriate gracious correction requires a community in which to work.

There is a further warning that I need to add here. While you can try to graciously reject a word that someone else provides, for correction to work properly, there are other characteristics that need to be cultivated in the community. A spirit of gossip can be destructive. Let's say that someone speaks a word to one person in private, and then they both share it with the pastor. The pastor may gently suggest listening more carefully for what God has said, and the two people leave. If one of them now gossips about the other, all the good work that the pastor has done can be undone by that simple act.

If there is a critical spirit active, then a sensitive person who is just learning to listen for the Lord's voice can be crushed. The spirit can be pervasive in a congregation, and make it *In order for the* impossible for people to learn to build their *gift of prophecy* communion with God because they know that *to work, there* someone is just waiting to jump on them for *must be an* every error that they might commit. *attitude of discernment, but* In order for the gift of prophecy or any type of *not of criticism.* speaking for God to work, there must be an attitude of discernment, but not of criticism, an attitude that permits one to give and receive rebuke, without giving or receiving condemnation. Those characteristics are not common in churches, but they should be actively cultivated.

GOD'S WORD IN AN IMPERFECT COMMUNITY

The fact is, of course, that we all live in imperfect communities, so I would like to suggest a better, more loving way to deal with God's word. **Don't make the claim; let others make the claim for you.** This doesn't mean that you shouldn't listen to God and accept what you believe you hear from the Lord. You should. Then you should test what you have heard and become as certain as you can that you are on the right track.

I personally have found that what I hear from the Lord in my devotional time almost always turns out to be simple wisdom once I have thought about it and prayed about it. This doesn't mean that there will never be "unusual" commands from God. Elijah's encounter on Mount Carmel, 450 Baal prophets against one man, didn't look like wisdom until the fire came down from heaven. But it was still God's command.

Yet the vast majority of God's commands are simply applications of divine principles and thus wise courses of action. Since they are wise things to do, you can explain the wisdom of them. Even if you believe fully that you got your idea directly from God, you can present the result on your own based on the logical and factual reasons why the idea is a good one.

Everything comes from God in the end, so he doesn't mind your presenting what you get from him as your own. If people ask you if you've prayed about it, you can honestly say that you have, but you don't have to claim divine authority. If others are practicing listening, and what you heard *is* from God, consensus is very likely to result.

The last person who must hear from God is you.

Reverse Manipulation

Sometimes when someone wants another person to accept what they have said, they will say, "Go pray about it, and see what God says."

Now the advice to "go pray about it" is generally good advice, but it can be used manipulatively. If I have already been praying about it, and believe that I have heard what I am going to hear from the Lord, then why is it that I need to go and pray some more?

Very frequently this is simply a tactic used by a dominant personality to push people who are less certain of their position into accepting what they say. The hearer begins to think, *He's a spiritual leader, and he must have been praying about this for a long time. Perhaps I'm wrong!*

Again, the answer is simple. The last person who must hear from God is you. Don't allow yourself to be spiritually bullied. Wait to hear from God for yourself, even if all you hear is that you should accept what another brother or sister has already said.

THE AUTHORITY OF INTERPRETATION

We have discussed the issue of testing the authority of those who claim the gift of prophecy and the ability to speak for God in that way. Many people claim that the safe thing to do is to reject all claims of prophecy and rely on the written word, the Bible.

But here we again encounter the issue of interpretation. Many teachers and preachers speak with great authority and then say, "This is not me speaking. I'm only telling you what the Bible says." But that assertion is always dangerous. When we apply the Bible to any particular situation we are interpreting. This is another case when one's words can seem very pious, but actually border on sacrilege.

The honest thing to do is to admit that what we say is our interpretation.

What could be more pious than simply speaking God's words and never adding anything of your own to them? But there is the problem. You and I are not capable of speaking "just what the Bible says." There is always something of our own thinking and interpretation in what we have to say.

The honest thing to do is to admit that what we say is our interpretation, and leave the accuracy of our interpretation open to discussion and discernment. At the same time, no matter how forcefully someone says that what they say is simply God's truth, whether they claim that they got it by hearing directly or by reading and interpreting sacred documents, discernment is always up to the individual hearer.

A word of prophecy must be tested. An interpretation of scripture must be tested. Everything must be tested using the intelligence God gives you and the wisdom he promises (James 1:5).

HEARING THE EXPRESSION

Many people have trouble enjoying the scriptures and finding power in and through them. They find that the written word is boring or incomprehensible, and so they don't get the benefit of the living word.

I want to present seven barriers to really hearing God's Word.[11] Break down these seven barriers and you will find that your experience of reading the Word will become more rewarding and will be a source of God's power in your life.

We lose the power and excitement of the Word when . . .

1. We don't know what the Word is.

God's Word is not limited to the written word. God created the universe through His Word (Psalm 33:6-9). Jesus was God's Word in human form (John 1:1-3, 14). God's Word is reflected throughout creation (Romans 1:20). The written word is God-breathed (2 Timothy 3:16, 17) and it is useful. The Word in all its forms is alive and active (Hebrews 4:12).

God's Word is not limited to the written word.

> *What God has said isn't only alive and active! It is sharper than any double-edged sword. His word can cut through our spirits and souls and through our joints and marrow, until it discovers the desires and thoughts of our hearts. - Hebrews 4:12 (CEV)*

---

11 The seven barriers are extracted from the Participatory Study Series pamphlet "Seven Barriers to Hearing God's Word," http://participatorystudyseries.com/pss_full_pamphlet.php?sku=PSS019.

If we come to the Bible understanding that we are reading a revelation from our creator and that his creative word is designed to transform us (2 Corinthians 5:17), we will find it hard to be bored!

2. We divorce the Word and the Spirit.

The original reception of the Word, our understanding of it, and its application are all brought about by the power of the Holy Spirit (2 Peter 1:19-21). When we separate the Word from the Spirit that gave it, it becomes a collection of dry facts. The Word should have the power to transform lives, but it can only do that when we allow it to work on our hearts and lives through the power of the Spirit.

The Word is not just a matter of reading, but of hearing and obedience.

> *Let me hear what God the LORD will speak,*
> *For he will speak peace to his people,*
> *To his faithful, to those who turn to him in their hearts.*
> *— Psalm 85:8 (NRSV)*

When we see the study of the Word as just a scholarly pursuit we will often study more about the Word than we study the Word itself.

3. We make the Word a scholarly rather than a spiritual study.

Scholarship is important in studying the Word, but we do not merely study in order to know facts; we study in order to know God. Further, we don't study to know about God; we study to know God.

When we see the study of the Word as just a scholarly pursuit we will often study more about the Word than we study the Word itself. Studying what others say about Scriptures can be valuable and is often necessary, but it is no substitute for studying the Word for yourself.

> *That's why only someone who has God's Spirit can understand spiritual blessings. Anyone who doesn't*

have God's Spirit thinks these blessings are foolish. People who are guided by the Spirit can make all kinds of judgments, but they cannot be judged by others. - 1 Corinthians 2:14, 15 (CEV)

4. We limit the study of the Word to a few rather than all.

The Bereans are commended for studying the Scriptures for themselves to see whether Paul's teachings were accurate (Acts 17:11). Jesus asked the young ruler how he read the scriptures (Luke 10:26). Part of the power of the Word is that God communicates with each one of us through it if we open our hearts to hear.

5. We limit the Word to church events, programs and curricula.

My soul is consumed with longing for your ordinances at all times. — Psalm 119:20 (NRSV)

Church members often leave teaching and learning the Word to church programs and events, sometimes because of laziness and sometimes just because they don't know how to study it or are afraid to study.

To make God's Word effective, we must "put everything to the test" and then accept the good and reject the evil.

If we are consumed with longing for God's Word at all times, then we will want to study it at home as well as at church or school. We will want to know for ourselves what it says and how it applies to our lives.

6. We lack discernment and courage to apply that discernment.

Don't turn away God's Spirit or ignore prophecies. Put everything to the test. Accept what is good and don't have anything to do with evil. - 1 Thessalonians 5:19-22 (CEV)

This applies especially to the spoken Word, but it also applies to any interpretation of the written Word.

We can destroy confidence in God's Word either by accepting everything as true without testing it, in which case people will lose confidence as false words or false interpretations cause destruction. We can also destroy God's Word by cutting off all words and interpretations.

To make God's Word effective, we must "put everything to the test" and then accept the good and reject the evil.

7. Lack of patience for hearing.

In Nehemiah's time, people listened to the Word for several hours (Nehemiah 8:1-8). We need patience to spend time listening to the Word and increasing our understanding of it. There are no shortcuts.

Recording – The Community Through Time

According to the chart on page 31 there are at least three elements that go into selection of a written work as authoritative:

1. It must be recognized as authentic.

2. It must be seen as having more than a local application.

3. It must be seen as being valuable for other times and circumstances than those of the original audience.

To be recognized as canonical a text must be seen as authentic and of broad applicability in time and location.

When all three of these elements are recognized in a piece of literature, it is likely that it will become canonical, that is, that it will be recognized by the community of faith as authoritative.

Before that can happen, however, it must be recorded and transmitted. Recording may take place in a number of ways. One way that is often not recognized in the modern world is simply memorization. People can memorize the words of the message and pass them on in that way to others. It is likely that early genealogies were preserved in this way, and it is also likely that some poetry was preserved by verbal memorization.

Rather than fully memorizing the words of a message, one can comprehend and assimilate the message, coming to understand its key points, and then to present those key points in one's own words later. This method of transmission applies most commonly to stories or to short sayings.

Form Criticism is the critical tool used by scholars to study oral transmission. Orally transmitted material tends to take on particular standard elements that provide a framework both for remembering and presenting the story or other element. When one starts a story "once upon a time" one is passing on a form, in this case most commonly used in fairy tales. Some of the identifiable forms in the Bible include parables (Matthew 13:24-30), etiological stories or legends (Genesis 22:14), and various forms of poetry (Psalm 29).

Orally transmitted material tends to take on particular standard elements that provide a framework both for remembering and presenting the story or other element.

One can subdivide these categories many times. The parable in Matthew 13:24-30 is specifically known as a "kingdom" parable, one in which Jesus will start "the kingdom of heaven is like." One can easily imagine early followers of Jesus thinking about what he had taught them, and asking themselves, "Just what all did Jesus say the kingdom of heaven is like?"

Poetry can be divided into prayers, hymns of praise, laments, and many others. Prophetic oracles, another form, are often presented in poetry. Psalm 29 is most commonly called a hymn of praise.

In modern charismatic groups I have seen prophecies, normally called "words from the Lord" passed on orally from person to person, sometimes to the extent that one can hardly recognize the end result. In many cases, however, these words will be recorded on tape, which is more reliable even than writing in providing an accurate record of something presented orally.

In other cases, the words will be written down, sometimes by the same person who spoke them, and sometimes by someone who heard. In one church, I encountered a number of notebooks in which various words from the Lord were recorded so that they could be referenced in later discussions.

Note that these texts did not become scripture, but nonetheless one could see part of the process of canonization taking place. Only words that were generally accepted by the congregation and leadership as coming from God were included. I never heard anyone challenge something that had already been recorded in the book. Further, only those words that applied to more than one person in the congregation were recorded. If you apply your imagination to this situation, you can see a small example of how something is recorded and preserved.

Items that apply to more than one person frequently are recorded in writing.

It's much easier to record the material today, but even in ancient times, the material generally got put into writing at some point. Of course for "scriptures," which means "writings," that is always true.

Writings can refer to many different things. They might refer to a letter that someone has written. Philemon, for example, is a personal letter that somehow became a part of scripture. Certainly that was due in part to the author, the apostle Paul. But one presumes that Paul wrote many things of which we have no record. This one personal letter had to be recognized as important, so that people would make copies of it and distribute it.

In other cases, we might have simple sayings, individual stories, or collections that are later brought together to produce a larger piece of literature. Proverbs identifies several collections, which have been brought together to form a larger book (Proverbs 1:1, 10:1, 25:1, 30:1, 31:1). It is quite likely that the various gospel writers copied from early collections of the sayings of Jesus, and also from one another in producing their own gospel story. Luke specifically mentions researching such things (Luke 1:1-4).

At a later date, others may look at the text, and add other materials to it. Comparing books like Samuel and Kings with Chronicles can give us an idea how someone might edit a book to produce a better final copy.

God provides equal, providential protection at all stages, but as in almost all aspects of our lives, he expects us first to use the tools and resources he has provided us.

THE IMPACT OF RECORDING AND TRANSMISSION

Many people are made very nervous by the idea of collecting, editing, and copying the words of scripture. How can these words remain accurate?

But how did the words get into human minds and onto human tongues in the first place? If one believes in divine inspiration of scriptures at all, one automatically believes in some level of miracles—of divine intervention in the world, however gently it is done.

So once we have assumed a miracle in the production of the initial message that God gave the prophet, we have no reason not to assume a similar miracle in the editing and transmission of the text.

We can set some boundaries on that miracle, however, in that we know that the methods of transmission do not provide 100% accuracy. If God protected the words as he gave them to the prophet in the first place, then why does he not protect them as they are transmitted? I would suggest that God provides equal, providential protection at all stages, but as in almost all aspects of our lives, he expects us first to use the tools and resources he has provided us.

BIBLICAL CRITICISM AND THE TRANSMISSION PROCESS

The historical-critical method is a scientific method of Bible study based on the assumption that there will be rational explanations for the text of scripture as we have it. As such, it is based on the ways in which we believe scripture has been transmitted to us. What we are trying to do with the historical-critical method is examine the way in which the scriptures got to us in the form in which we have them.

The basic assumption of the method is that there are human authors who use oral traditions and textual sources and compose texts in the way that other authors do.

The mind of an understanding person seeks knowledge. - Proverbs 15:14 (HN)

It is not necessary to assume that there is no supernatural involvement in order to use the historical-critical method. One simply has to give the human agents some freedom in the way that they worked. The scriptures themselves provide us with adequate evidence of different personalities and circumstances of writing and transmission having an impact on the final product.[12]

While the historical-critical method looks for natural explanations, it is not necessary to assume that there is no supernatural involvement in producing the Biblical text. It is necessary to look for natural methods as the primary mode of producing the text.

_____

12 Often using critical methodologies without naturalistic assumptions is called "historical-contextual" study, but I see no reason to assume that one must make naturalistic assumptions in order to use the historical-critical method. One's specific results may differ greatly, however, and one's application will certainly do so.

Basics of the Historical-Critical Method

What Happened in History	Stage	How We Study It
	Jesus uses parables (example, parable of the sower, Matthew 1:3-9)	
Various hearers repeat the parable to one another, possibly for more than one generation, for example person A tells it to person B who then tells person C and so forth.		Form Criticism
	An oral tradition exists of what Jesus said.	
The collection of parables is written down and circulates apart from any gospel—all the parables in Matthew 13, for example.		Source Criticism
	A written collection of parables is in circulation.	
An author takes the collection of parables, other collections of sayings or deeds, and information from his own knowledge and creates a final gospel text, putting the material in order, placing emphasis on certain topics, creating transitions and modifying specific vocabulary to fit his themes.[1]		Redaction Criticism
	A final gospel text (Matthew)	
Matthew is copied by hand many times, with some copies preserved. Different copies contain different errors.		Textual Criticism
	A copy of the Greek text of Matthew is prepared for a translator, such as in a modern Greek New Testament.	

[1] The parables are commonly thought to have been collected first in Mark or in a source before Mark, and then copied to Matthew and Luke. There were some independent parables. (Luke 16, for example).

If you assume that the words of scripture were dictated by God through the Biblical writers, and thus the entire text is produced directly by supernatural processes, then the critical methodologies would not be applicable. Oral transmission, use of source documents and editing are all not compatible with direct divine dictation.

But the evidence of scripture itself suggests that while God inspired the message, there is a substantial role for natural processes. Some stories, sayings, prophetic oracles parables were transmitted from person to person orally before being written. The books of Joshua, Judges, Samuel and Kings refer to other written sources, such as the book of Jasher (Joshua 10:13, 2 Samuel 1:18) and the books of the chronicles of the kings of Judah and also of Israel. The books show the personalities of different authors, and the characteristics of their time and place.

Those who use historical-critical methodologies tend to be more willing to speculate.

Thus these critical methodologies are of use in a serious study of scripture. We must be careful, however, with our assumptions. If we read that a certain event could not have taken place as written because a miracle is required, we need to be aware of the assumption behind that statement. If a prediction is dated to after the event it predicts because no prediction is possible, again, we must be aware of the assumption behind this statement as well.

On the other hand, critical methodology can help keep us from assuming miracles that the scriptures themselves do not claim. Such claims can simply make our faith look silly. We need to be careful with making claims of miracles that are greater than what scripture itself asserts.

RELATING INSPIRATION TO BIBLICAL CRITICISM

There are a variety of views of inspiration. Of these views, those that hold to any type of verbal dictation, the view that the very words of scripture were dictated by God, would be incompatible with the historical critical method.

Others will find that the various critical methodologies are helpful in learning to understand the text of scripture. Some of these methods are used in the historical-contextual study. The primary difference is one of perspective rather than a fundamental methodology. Those who hold to the contextual method are generally more conservative in their approach and in their conclusions, and generally are more concerned with the final form of the text of scripture. Those who use historical-critical methodologies tend to be more willing to speculate. They are also more concerned with the process by which scripture got to its present form, and sometimes study the process to the exclusion of the product—the Bible as we have it..

Many historical-critical methodologies address the process by which scripture was produced more than the final product.

Those who take a high view of scripture, including those who accept the Chicago Statement on Biblical Inerrancy use various of the methods that are part of the historical-critical method. Clearly there will be differences in how one will use these methods depending on one's view of the role of divine inspiration in the production of the text.

METHODS THAT TAKE A BROADER LOOK

Literary criticism looks at the document as a piece of literature. Tradition criticism looks at the whole of the process of transmission, and canonical criticism which examines the scriptural text in its final (or canonical) form. Rhetorical criticism looks at the genre of broader sections of scripture, asking, for example, what type of literature a "gospel" is, and what are its characteristics.[13]

---

13 The use of the term **genre** differs in form criticism, which deals with small portions transmitted orally, and in **genre criticism**, which tends to deal with larger documents.

SPECULATION AND EVIDENCE IN BIBLICAL CRITICISM

As in any field, many critical theories about the text of the Bible are speculative, and each should be understood and evaluated based on the amount of evidence supporting it.

A good practice is never to come to a conclusion about any issue without reading more than one source. Often authors express doubtful conclusions with great confidence, either because they are more sure of themselves than they ought to be, or because they hope that people won't question them because of their assurance.

Be very wary of this tactic when used on any side of a debate. Those who use critical methodologies often sneer at those who don't, or at those whose theories are less radical than their own, as less intelligent, backwards, or ignorant. Conservative critics of the historical critical methodology often accuse their opponents of a lack of faith or a desire to tear down the faith of others.

Many critical theories about the text of the Bible are speculative, and each should be understood and evaluated based on the amount of evidence supporting it.

You should look past such accusations and examine the evidence. Christians have nothing to fear from studying evidence openly, and we have every reason to want people to openly search for truth.

"HIGHER CRITICISM" AND "LOWER CRITICISM"

Biblical criticism-the critical study of the Bible-involves a number of methods that we have already discussed. The method most solidly based on physical evidence is textual criticism, which is the comparison of various copies to find the most likely original text. Textual criticism was established before most of the other methods, such as form, redaction, source and literary criticism that study the authorship and the history of the text before it was made into a final edition which was then copied.

When the newer methods were first invented people needed a way to distinguish these new, more controversial approaches to Bible study from the well established idea of textual criticism. Thus the label "higher criticism" was born, and "lower criticism" was invented in reaction to describe the existing textual criticism.

CANONICITY

Many people think about the terms "inspired" and "canonical" as nearly synonymous. Generally they are not.

It would be hard to force a community to accept as authoritative material that they truly did not like.

The term "canon" relates to idea of canon law, in other words a book is canonical when canon laws defines it as authoritative. Now the edges have become blurred over the years, and we have many different churches, but in general you will still find a statement in any church's statement of beliefs that designates certain books of the Bible as canonical. For protestant churches, this is almost always the 66 books that have been accepted as canonical by protestants since the protestant reformation. The Roman Catholic Church, various eastern Orthodox churches and some smaller bodies have different lists of books.

The books listed as canonical are generally assumed to be inspired, and thus to carry divine authority. But the act of making certain books canonical does not necessarily make them the only books that are inspired by God. Other works may be inspired, and individuals or groups may regard other works as authoritative.

Some people will tell you that they have a "personal canon," a set of books that they regard as authoritative. In one sense, that is a contradiction in terms, since "canon" by nature involves a community to which the standard applies, and not an individual. In some cases, rather than authoritative, those who use this term mean their personal list of books that are inspired. I prefer not to use that second sense, because it reinforces the notion that "canonical" and "inspired" are synonyms.

The way in which a canon of literature is established depends on the type of community that establishes it. Since we are dealing with the Christian community, let's consider first how the early church went about it. It was, in many ways a contest of popularity, though of a very special kind. The larger the number of churches and church leaders who used a book as authoritative, the more likely it was to be accepted by the councils.

There is thus no surprise that the same councils that defined what it meant to be orthodox would also produce a canon of scripture that would tend to support their orthodox position.

I don't mean by this that the process was cynical. People genuinely believed themselves to be led by God in their choices, and by accepting the Christian canon, I acknowledge that leadership. In practice it would be hard to force a community to accept as authoritative material that they truly did not like. It would, in fact, be very inconsistent of the councils to accept one set of doctrinal standards and then choose a Biblical canon that opposed that position.

It is no more difficult for God to guide the process of canonization than it is for him to guide the original writing process.

How does this relate to inspiration? Many people see the process of canonization as a major problem for Christian scripture. Shouldn't there be some obvious way of know what is scripture and what is not? Well, there was no obvious way to know that a book was inspired in the first place. That knowledge was the result of testing and discernment.

Consider Jeremiah preaching in Jerusalem. Outside are Babylonian troops. How do you know whether Jeremiah is a true prophet or not? When Baruch, Jeremiah's scribe, writes the message, do you immediately know this is a sacred text that will have authority in the community of faith for thousands of years? You don't. You have to decide what to do without all of that knowledge. Will you follow Jeremiah's advice and go out to the Babylonians, or will you follow the king and his prophets and stay in the city? Your life depends on the right answer!

Inherent in the way Gandhi inspired people to action was the fact that he angered other people.

The key thing to remember here is that it is no more difficult for God to guide the process of canonization than it is for him to guide the original writing process. In addition, the intervening time allows people to study the text and apply their knowledge and discernment. The result is that the decision about inspiration is much easier at the time of canonization than it is at the time the word is first heard.

Very frequently a community later accepts as authoritative someone who was not popular in his own time. Jeremiah is an excellent example. He was persecuted when he spoke, his work was cut up when he wrote, and he ended up forcibly taken to Egypt against his will. But his book later became an authoritative part of scripture.

This leads me to point out a near contradiction between immediate inspiration and immediate relevance of a message and its acceptance as canonical. Some of the most inspired and challenging statements that have ever been made have been given to communities that rejected them. I suspect that in most times the message of a true prophet will not be well received. A message may evoke a very mixed reception.

Gandhi was poorly received by the British occupiers and by those who wanted to turn to violence. Others received his work joyfully.

Inherent in the way he inspired people to action was the fact that he angered other people.

But simply asking whether a work is canonical or not is not a very good way to determine its value to your own spiritual life. Most of the material we now have in the Bible and which is regarded by all Christian churches as authoritative, was once poorly received by at least a part of the community. The things that truly correct us and call us to greater action are likely to be frowned upon by those who need them most.

What a defined canon does for us is tell us what defines our community. It does not define the boundaries of what helps us grow spiritually.[14]

MODERN ADDITIONS TO THE CANON

One person peppered me with Ellen White quotations even though she knew I was no longer a church member. She then offered to send me a compilation of even more such statements.

Because I grew up in the Seventh-day Adventist (SDA) Church, I have had a lifelong interest in modern prophetic writings and their authority in particular communities. SDAs have Ellen G. White whose voluminous writings are regarded as authoritative by the vast majority of church members. They would not call this an addition to the canon of scripture, though with many it is hard to tell the difference. After I was no longer an SDA myself, I recall getting involved in the peripheries of an argument. One person peppered me with Ellen White quotations even though she knew I was no longer a church member. She then offered to send me a compilation of even more such statements. She treated Ellen White as part of the canon, not only authoritative for her personally, but also for me.

---

14 An excellent short overview of the canon can be found in Smith, T. C. How We God Our Bible. Macon, GA: Smyth & Helwys Publishing, 1994.

The Church of Jesus Christ of Latter Day Saints (Mormons) not only hold that additional books are inspired, but tend to see them as having effectively greater authority than the Bible. Again, in conversation Mormons have told me that they do regard the Bible as the key authority, and other works as providing additional interpretation and application. Yet in practice they allow the more modern works to substantially alter or define the text of the Bible. At a minimum I would expect that working from a Biblical base would involve using the best evidence of what the Bible said. Allowing another book to redefine the Bible suggests that the second book is effectively of greater authority.

Turning again to SDAs, though they do not let Ellen White define the text of scripture, I was frequently asked to view Ellen White's interpretation as definitive. (Note that this was not a common practice amongst SDA academics.)

The entire process of interpretation must be accessible to all.

It is not my intent here to criticize either group as such, but rather to point out the practice and express this principle: Whatever you take as the final authority on interpretation or content is actually your final authority for understanding. This can be the teaching authority of the church as in the Catholic tradition. It can be a modern prophet. It can also be the practice of modern prophecy in the church. I have heard people who were called prophets proclaim interpretations of scripture that were clearly contrary to what the Bible writer was actually intending to express, yet their congregations would take such interpretations as final truth, not to be challenged.

Unless you personally can go back to the original source and challenge the new interpretation, it is the new interpretation that is being given final authority. This does not mean that no new interpretation can ever be accepted. It means that the entire process of interpretation must be accessible to all, and that each person must go back to the authority and check the result.

That is the importance of the Biblical canon in Christianity. It is a single, central source of authority, acknowledged by the vast majority of Christians. Thus it can be used in discussions regardless of denomination. Though there are some differences between protestant, Catholic, and eastern canons, these only have a minor impact.

Provided that such modern writings as a group regards as inspired are not used as the final authority, they do not interfere.[15] But the church is not in unity at this time so as to have a general council and accept some new piece of writing as canonical.

---

15 As I understand it, the official SDA position does not place Ellen White on a level with canonical scripture, while the Mormon view does place the Book of Mormon in that position. It is not, however, my intent to discuss these groups specifically, but rather the principles involved.

TRANSLATION

For a community like the Christian community that is extended both in geography and in time, once a message is initially recorded it may have to be translated. For purposes of discussion, I want to distinguish two processes. First, there is the transfer of the message from one language into another, with the intension of conveying the verbal message into another language. Second, there is the transformation of the basic message so that it can be presented in different ways, while keeping its integrity as a message.

Even the most literal translations do not manage a word-by-word equivalence

VERBAL TRANSLATION

Many people connect one's idea of inspiration with one's approach to translation. The assumption seems to be that a person who believes in some form of verbal inspiration, especially verbal plenary inspiration, will necessarily favor a formal, word-by-word, or literal translation. Of these terms I prefer formal, in that even the most literal translations do not manage a word-by-word equivalence, but rather account for the grammatical form and structure of the source language in the form and structure of the text in the receptor language as far as possible.

My own position on translation reflects the same relationship. I reject verbal dictation or even verbal plenary inspiration, and I believe in dynamic equivalence. But it would be a mistake to assume that these preferences are universal. Normally there are two extremes in focus for a translator. He may either think primarily about communication, how easily the message can be understood, or about reflecting the source text, it's style, time, and culture. If he prefers the former, he will prefer a dynamic equivalence translation. If the latter, he will probably prefer formal equivalence. In practice all translators are concerned with both elements, but in different proportions.

I believe God inspires messengers with messages through various experiences, rather than dictating words.

My non-verbal view of inspiration means that I believe God inspires messengers with messages through various experiences, rather than dictating words, though the message may include a verbally dictated component. In Ezekiel 1 for example, my understanding is that God presented Ezekiel with a vision and Ezekiel searched for the words with which to present what he had seen, accounting for the slightly confused nature of the text. In a translation I would like to convey the message that Ezekiel tried to present, and I would also like to maintain some of the emotional tension that the style of writing conveys.

In actual practice, I have found that many translators that I know accept verbal plenary inspiration, and nonetheless support the same approach to translation that I do. I have encountered numerous people whose view of inspiration is more liberal than my own, including some people who have no belief in the Bible at all, who prefer a more formal approach to translation. This is usually because they like to see as much as possible of the source language characteristics reflected in the translation.

What I have never found is anyone who wants a translation to be inaccurate, though I suppose some such person must exist somewhere. No matter what their view of scripture, if they read it at all they want to know what it actually says.

There is a distinction in the way each person views *accuracy*. There seem to be two views. First, accuracy can be conceived as an attribute of the text apart from the process of communication. Alternatively, accuracy can be seen as pertaining only to the entire process of communication.

Let me clarify one point. Accuracy *is* an attribute of the text, i.e. you can have an extremely clear text that is quite inaccurate, and an accurate text that is incomprehensible to some people. But if a text is intended to communicate, and pretty generally they are, then one cannot speak of the accuracy of communication without looking at whether the intended audience can understand the text.

However much "accuracy" I may attribute to the text in the abstract, in an actual situation of communication, a word that is not understood cannot be accurate.

When somebody tells me the word "justify" is the most accurate translation for Greek forms of the word "δικαιοω" I have to immediately ask, "Accurate to whom?" It would not be the most accurate word to use for a Spanish speaking audience. One may object that we're talking about an English speaking audience because "justify" is an English word. But is anyone naive enough to suppose that there are not dialects of English? In fact, "justify" communicates well to some people, and poorly to others. However much "accuracy" I may attribute to the text in the abstract, in an actual situation of communication, a word that is not understood cannot be accurate.

This is critical distinction. People who are most concerned with *communicating the message of scripture* are most likely to support dynamic equivalence in translation, whether or not they support a form of verbal inspiration. Of course very few people will admit that they are not interested in communication. We gather that it is not their primary focus, however, when they suggest that people should learn the difficult terms often included in church language, or that they should become accustomed to characteristics of the source language. If they must do that, there is a barrier between them and God's word in scripture.

Why should I use another word or even an explanatory phrase for "justify" when the target audience can be forced to learn how to understand what "justify" means? Let them come to the Bible! Let's not "dumb down" the Bible. But in fact they are not being required to come to the Bible, but rather to a specific form in which the Bible's message is expressed. Restating the Bible in the dialect of the target audience is not "dumbing down." It's simply accurate translation *when translation is viewed in the context of communicating the message to a particular audience.*

To force a particular vocabulary on people before they can receive the message of the gospel is to put a stumbling block in front of people.

This is why it's so important to make the distinction between the Greek, Hebrew, or Aramaic text and the English text that is translated from it. Somebody has to learn the words in which scripture was originally given. Very few people need to learn a particular set of words into which scripture has been translated. The act of translating a particular Greek word by a particular English word does not forever privilege that word.

It strikes me that forcing a particular vocabulary on people before they can receive the message of the gospel is putting a stumbling block in front of people. We make them learn our church language before they can hear the message that Jesus intended to present.

An Example: Choosing the ESV

The following example comes from a recent discussion amongst various blogs. It provides an example of the issues involved in the choice of a Bible translation for a church.

I have heard many good things about Mars Hill Church in Seattle, despite some theological disagreements (with whom do I not have such disagreements?). Recently a friend sent me a link to: *Theological reasons for why Mars Hill preaches out of the ESV.*[16]

This isn't intended as an attack on the ESV. On the cover of my book *What's in a Version?*[17], I put the slogan "the best Bible version is one you read." If you find your Bible reading life lighting up when you read the ESV, then by all means use it for reading and study. If the carefully gender accurate language of such versions as the NRSV grates on your nerves, then by all means use the ESV, but admit that it's because of your language tastes, and not because of theology. If you're reading the ESV because you think it is theologically more correct, or because it more accurately and clearly conveys the message of scripture to the populace in general, then I urge you to think again.

> *If God inspired the very words and details, he did not do so in English.*

The stated fundamental assumption is one of inspiration. I don't agree with the Mars Hill stand on Biblical inspiration, but I'm not going to dispute that. Rather, I want to ask if their stand on inspiration does really underly the remainder of their statement, or whether it actually stands on something else—something much less well founded. I quote:

---

16 From http://www.marshillchurch.org/content/ESVtheologicalreasons, last accessed 4/10/07.
17 Neufeld, Henry. What's in a Version? Gonzalez, FL: Energion Publications, 2005.

1. The ESV upholds the truth that Scripture is the very words of God, not just the thoughts of God.

This point is inextricably connected to the doctrine of verbal plenary inspiration, which means that God the Holy Spirit inspired not just the thoughts of Scripture but the very words and details. . . .

Now here's the problem. If God inspired the very words and details, he did not do so in English. He did so in Hebrew, Aramaic, and Greek. I have no problem with this, but then I don't believe in verbal plenary inspiration. It is obvious that in translation one **must** without exception alter the "words and details" of the source text, for the simple reason that an English translation contains no words in Hebrew, Aramaic, or Greek, with the exception of a few transliterations. One assumes that Pastor Mark Driscoll is aware of this fact, but he glosses over it, as do most advocates of literal, word for word translation.

A pastor or teacher may have become used to using one word rather than another, but that doesn't make the earlier word more accurate, nor the new word an alteration.

The practice actually reflects an argument used for many years by KJV Only advocates, who compare every new version to the KJV, and then call every change *from the KJV* in a modern version a change in the scriptures. They accuse the modern versions of altering the words of scripture. But what words are altered? The words of a translation that has no authority whatsoever over the source texts. When a translator uses a word/phrase in the receptor language to reflect a word/phrase in the source language, that doesn't make the two equivalent. It is simply the way that translator thought was best to convey the *thought* of the text in the source language in the receptor language. It is critically important to state this correctly: **The translator(s) of a new Bible** translation do not alter the words of scripture, they reflect the words of scripture in a different way, using different words.

To illustrate, let's go back to the illustration of the Greek word "δικαιοω." If one translation uses "justify" and then a newer translation uses "make right with God," neither translation alters the words of scripture. They simply present those words in a different way. A pastor or teacher may have become used to using one word rather than another, but that doesn't make the earlier word more accurate, nor the new word an alteration. It is often inconvenient to communicate accurately, but it is necessary nonetheless.

Some people are going to think I'm being unfair, but stripped of all the extra verbiage, Pastor Mark Driscoll's argument is, in fact, no more sophisticated than the KJV Only argument on this point. Let's look at some illustrations. Point 4 says "The ESV upholds the theological nomenclature of Scripture." Exactly how does it do this? Does it use the Greek nomenclature? That was the nomenclature of scripture. No English word can justify the title "nomenclature of scripture."

If one translation uses "justify" and then a newer translation uses "make right with God," neither translation alters the words of scripture.

Driscoll settles in on just that word—justify. Because it is so central to the reformation and has been fought over so much, and so many people have died for it, it must be a special, sacred word. But again, very few of the people who died over this concept during the reformation died over the words "justify" or "justification." Sometimes they used the Greek word, sometimes the Latin, and sometimes whatever word was most appropriate in their native language. In English, that was the word "justify" and its cognate "justification" because those were the words used in translation. Now we have the complaint that dynamic equivalence translations, such as the CEV, NLT, and The Message don't use the word justify.

Instead, horror of horrors, they use other English words or even phrases to express the concept of justification to the modern audience. They are no more changing the words of scripture than were the KJV translators when they used justify, or when Martin Luther used "gerecht werden" in Romans 3:24.

Thus Driscoll's comment that some of these versions are more writing commentary than scripture. What they, or anyone who reads any translation are doing is reading the words that the translators chose in order to represent the original languages in what they thought was the best way.[18]

If inspiration consists of words and details, then it is simply impossible, without exception, for a translation to convey those words and details.

This is simply so naive that I have difficulty believing it was written by someone with Mark Driscoll's training and writing skills. The word "justification" is not in the "words and details" of scripture as inspired by God. There is a Greek word in that verse. Early translators into English chose to translate that word with the English word "justify" and its various cognates. Justify became part of the "churchese" dictionary, and presumably is part of the dialect spoken at Mars Hill Church. But no amount of theological claims will make "justify" the actual inspired word. *None* of the translations quoted say "what God and the Holy Spirit said through Paul" under the standard that Driscoll is presenting.

If inspiration consists of words and details, then it is simply impossible, without exception, for a translation to convey those words and details. It can't be done. Now one can carefully study those words and details, discover what thoughts they reflect, and express those thoughts in the receptor language. But that is apparently not good enough for Driscoll. He wants "what God and the Holy Spirit said through Paul." But he has skipped a few steps of the logic in getting to his claim that the ESV better reflects that than

---

18 Driscoll, op cit.

do the translations he decries. The only reason "justify" is somehow considered Paul's word selection is because it was attached to the Greek word "δικαιοω" by early translators, and it has become equivalent in his mind. *But it is not equivalent. It is still an English word with English semantic range.*

Let's go back to point #2: "The ESV upholds that what is said must be known before what is meant can be determined." Again, this is an astounding statement, but one regularly made by advocates of literal translation. I think that Hebrew and Greek training in seminaries is partially responsible. Students are regularly taught to gloss their translations very literally, often with the explanation that they don't know enough Greek or Hebrew yet to be a bit less literal, but in most cases they never get to the point of translating the meaning with accuracy into good English (or other receptor language). Thus much of what passes for exegesis based on the Hebrew and Greek from Christian pulpits is actually founded on a schoolbook idea of translation. (By "gloss" I mean providing a word or set of words to replace the single expression in the source language, rather than defining the word(s) and then providing a meaningful and natural translation.) I'm as guilty as the next person on this point, and I believe I need to improve on teaching Biblical languages students about language, and not just teaching them essentially how other people have translated.

Words carry meaning, but they are not the sole carriers of meaning.

Point #3 is equally naive: "The ESV upholds the truth that words carry meaning." Of course, words carry meaning, but they are not the sole carriers of meaning. There are numerous cases in which a word means something completely different in a particular idiomatic expression or in a particular syntactic structure. An excessively literal translation can easily miss these nuances while providing "accurate" glosses for the individual words. Meaning is carried at many levels in a text, and not just the words.

Under point #5, we repeat this error: "However, we must remember that we cannot change the words of Scripture because God has called us to not only communicate widely, but also communicate truthfully." *But we change the words in all cases!* The only question is how accurately we communicate the *message.*

I must add a note in response to point #5. It reads: "The ESV upholds the truth that while Scripture is meant for all people, it cannot be communicated in such a way that all people receive it." In one sense, we know that this is true–not everyone receives the word, and certainly not everyone comprehends it. But is that an excuse for failing to communicate as accurately as possible? Would anyone make the argument that the Holy Spirit wants us to obscure the meaning to our audience because some of them won't understand it anyhow? I think that would be like a fireman saying that some of those trapped in a burning building are going to die, so he doesn't need to bother to rescue as many as possible. It sounds to me like putting a stumbling block in front of people. Personally, I don't want someone's rejection of the gospel to come because I communicated it ineffectively. I know that I'm going to fail at times, and I know that some people will refuse to understand, but I never want either of those things to happen because I decided it just didn't matter that much.

Would anyone make the argument that the Holy Spirit wants us to obscure the meaning to our audience because some of them won't understand it anyhow?

Then of course we have to have point #6: "The ESV upholds the complementarian nature of gender in Scripture." The whole idea of the complementarian nature of gender is built on some very odd views of language. "Male representation," for example, is a completely unfounded structure designed solely to make certain scriptures mean things that the *words* do not indicate. It's interesting that it is an argument presented largely by those who focus on the meaning of the *words,* as opposed to broader structures.

In support of this Driscoll makes another set of statements that strike me with awe in their inaccuracy.

It must be pointed out that, in its more insidious forms, the push for gender-neutral language is in fact a clear push against Scripture. For example, Scripture states that God made us "male and female" (for example, Genesis 1:27). Consequently, in God's created order, there is both equality between men and women (because both are His image-bearers) and distinction (because men and women have differing roles). This position is called complementarianism and teaches that men and women, though equal, are also different in some ways and therefore function best together in a complementary way, like a right hand and left hand (1 Corinthians 11:3; Ephesians 5:22–33; Colossians 3:18–19; 1 Timothy 2:8–3:13). But those with a feminist and/or homosexual agenda are seeking to eradicate the created distinction between males and females so as to validate new alternative lifestyles that are not acceptable according to Scripture. Translations such as the New Revised Standard accommodate this by wrongly translating "male and female" in Genesis 1:27 as the androgynous "humankind." The New Living Bible translates it as the genderless "people." There are many reasons why all of this matters to Bible translation.[19]

If they truly believe that one must not alter the words and details of scripture in any way, then they must logically begin to use only the texts in the source languages.

Now look at the translation of Genesis 1:27 in the criticized NRSV:

---

19 Driscoll, op cit.

27 So God created humankind in his image,
in the image of God he created them;
male and female he created them. — Genesis 1:27
(NRSV)

Hold it! There's "male and female" right there. So what did the NRSV alter? They altered not one single word of scripture more than did the ESV. The simply translated Hebrew "'adam" as "humankind" rather than as "man." That is, like the NLT's "people," a more accurate translation into current English than is "man." The reason for the objection goes back to that old KJV Only argument–the word as chosen by the KJV translators was "man" so "man" it is, even though the word "man" does not, of course, appear in the source texts.

The world often reads only the message as portrayed by the people who claim to be following it.

My concern here is not that Mars Hill Church is using a bad translation, but rather that they are advocating this position with a set of arguments that are completely fallacious. This will lead people to make bad decisions on Bible translations, assuming all the time that they have sound theological backing.

In fact, their conclusions are not based on their own arguments. If they truly believe in "verbal plenary inspiration" and believe that one must not alter the words and details of scripture in any way, then they must logically begin to use only the texts in the source languages. Sunday School classes should start with programs in Biblical languages. But if they once admit that the meaning of the source languages can be transferred, even if only partially, into a receptor language, then they must also admit that one can change the words, because *every translation changes the words*. If they want to make the word choice of the KJV the standard, even only of certain theological terms, then they need to explain why those particular word choices are privileged over others. (Note, of course, that many of the KJV word choices were taken from prior English translations.)

I would not even respond to a church's choice of translation if they presented it as just their choice based on *preference*. You can use what you wish based on your taste, and if it works for you and communicates the message adequately, then blessings on you! Go, read, do! But if you base your choice on failed linguistic arguments, and present it as somehow a choice that is closer to the pure gospel than others, then it's time to respond.

TRANSFORMING THE MESSAGE

It's easy to ignore another aspect of translating a message. When a message is received it will generally have results, and those results are, themselves, a form of translation.

Imagine a multinational army that must pass orders to various elements. As these orders are received by various units, they would have to be translated into a language that the soldiers of that unit understood. That's the paper translation.

God's Spirit works in very human instruments to produce a very human book that is divinely inspired and inspiring.

But all units, irrespective of language, have to translate the contents of those orders into language. This translation is seen as the units move into the positions they have been ordered to take, undertake fire missions, send out patrols, and so forth.

If one wanted to study the history of that battle, it would be quite appropriate to research files of the orders and translations. It would also be appropriate to check on what the soldiers actually did. Either one would give you some insight into the orders as originally written, though you could never be certain that a particular unit had carried out its orders correctly.

In the case of the Christian message, that translation of the orders into action takes place in the Christian community, and much like our hypothetical army, the actual translation varies in its accuracy. The world often reads only the message as portrayed by the people who claim to be following it. That is the other side of translation—the type of translation that goes on all the time in your life and mine.

Which translation do you think is more important?

AN INCARNATIONAL VIEW OF INSPIRATION AND TRANSLATION

"Dynamic equivalence,"– trying to produce the same effect in a modern audience that the original text (or spoken words) would have produced in their original audience– that's a worthy, fire-in-the-bones goal.

Now let's try to look at a more positive view of inspiration and how it might relate to translation.

When I read the Bible I am struck regularly by two things. First, I am driven to come closer to God through what I read, thus I feel the inspiration of scripture in action. Second, I regularly notice the personality, literary style, and even the theology of the individual authors.

I call this the incarnational view of inspiration.[20] God's Spirit works in very human instruments to produce a very human book that is divinely inspired and inspiring. The text becomes a medium for the working of the Holy Spirit.

My question is this: How does this impact the way we translate? What translation principles are best suited to translating such a book?

I'm tempted to answer simply that if the Bible is fully human (without denying that it's fully divine), then our translation principles

---

20 I'm indebted for the phrase "incarnational view of inspiration" to Alden Thompson, Inspiration: Hard Questions, Honest Answers. Hagerstown, MD: Review and Herald Publishing Association, 1991, pp. 87-97.

should be the same as they are for any other fully human book. A translation should be clear, accurate, and natural.[21]

But just as the divine side of Jesus (holy, blameless, undefiled–Hebrews 7:26) draws us away from the failures and the weaknesses and "leads us on toward perfection" (Hebrews 6:1), so I would suggest that our belief in the divine side of scripture should draw us forward toward the best translation effort possible. That best effort, in my view, should be to let the modern reader or hearer *hear God* in the human language of scripture.

I have never accepted the notion that one must be skilled in the source languages in order to understand the Bible.

That's why I like the term "dynamic equivalence" even over more current terms like "functional equivalence." Don't get me wrong. Functional equivalence is a good and descriptive term, but it somehow fails to become a fire in my bones. "Dynamic equivalence,"–trying to produce the same effect in a modern audience that the original text (or spoken words) would have produced in their original audience[22]–that's a worthy, fire-in-the-bones goal.

I have never actually seen it, though there are passages in numerous versions that do approach it. It's a bit like the "perfection" of Hebrews 6:1–you keep moving toward it. It's the north star, drawing

---

21 I got the phrase "clear, accurate, and natural" from Wayne Leman of the Better Bibles Blog (http://englishbibles.blogspot.com) in various internet communications.

22 I was first introduced to dynamic equivalence in the following passage: "In such a translation [dynamic equivalence] one is not so concerned with matching the receptor-language message with the source-language message, but with the dynamic relationship, . . . that the relationship between receptor and message should be the same as that which existed between the original receptors and the message." Nida, Eugene. Toward a Science of Translating. Leiden, E. J. Brill, 1964. p. 159. I have been in love with the concept ever since I read it.

you toward it, but light years away. I have never myself produced anything that I even regard as a *good* translation in writing. They're just adequate to their purpose most of the time.

I recall one instance on a mission trip when I was asked to give a devotional. Because I had heard some team members talking about how they were less spiritual than others, and that the officially religious folks (myself included) were doing the "spiritual work," I used a portion of 1 Corinthians 12. I read it over and over from my Greek Testament until it was rooted in me, and then I just spoke my translation from my heart. I recommended that members of the team read the passage for themselves. One member came to me after the devotional time and said, "What translation were you reading from? I want to read it in *that* translation."

God "got into" the words in Hebrew and Greek, and I think that with the aid of the Holy Spirit, he can "get into" the words in English.

I wish I could produce that effect on demand, but I can't. Even at that, of course, it was only a translation *going on toward perfection*, not one that had attained it. I'm guessing that the only way to do it would be to spend as much time with each passage, under as much conviction of the Holy Spirit as I was under at that time, before letting the passage pour forth for your audience as God's message for God's people on God's mission.

Even though I studied Biblical languages in school, I have never accepted the notion that one must be skilled in the source languages in order to understand the Bible. I suspect this comes from my incarnational view as well. God "got into" the words in Hebrew and Greek, and I think that with the aid of the Holy Spirit, he can "get into" the words in English.

Translators, teachers, and expositors also become the conduit for God's power in God's word to get to God's people. That's the guiding star, I think, of truly dynamic–filled with dunamis–Bible translation.

AUTHORITY AND TRUTH

One of the key differences between theology and science is that science expects to change, whereas if theology is not assuming it is founded on bedrock, it is at least looking for some bedrock. Religious people often criticize science on the basis that it changes too often. Its history is one of repeatedly overturned theories. Scientists, however, will tell you this is the great strength of science, and rightfully so.

A scientific heretic has one simple thing to do: Amass the evidence to support his or her theory.

A scientific heretic has one simple thing to do: Amass the evidence to support his or her theory. The more deeply embedded the opposing view is in scientific thinking the more evidence and reasoning will be required to overturn it. Theories such as Wegener's proposal on continental drift can take years, but scientific theories are not impregnable.

This scientific resistance to heresies is often cited as a weakness of science, and indeed previous paradigms can be very dangerous to the process of discovery and growth of knowledge. But such scientific theories gain their place in thinking not merely because of age, but because they have proven useful repeatedly, and data from various areas fit with them.

In theology, on the other hand, our doctrines don't have a working test. We cannot produce statistics, for example, on how many people have gone to heaven or hell, or even on the potentially easier subject of how many prayers are answered and in what way.[23] In fact for many people in many different religions, the age of an idea is the primary test of its veracity, which presents a great difficulty for progressive religion. In progressive Christianity, interpretation of the Bible and a view of church tradition frequently combine to make war on new ideas of any type. In order to be progressive, many people assume they must discard the Bible.

Heresy of doctrinal standards defined by your religious organization. Because science and theology have fundamentally different approaches their idea of heresy is different as well. In religion, heresy is a failure to abide by a set of doctrinal standards defined by your religious organization. I'm not at all worried about being a Muslim heretic simply because I'm not a Muslim. One can only cease being a heretic by bringing oneself into line with those standards.

A scientific "heretic," on the other hand, is not one who violates some kind of written code of ancient teaching or a set of doctrines of his organization. The response of science is not to conduct heresy trials, but to demand evidence. In practice, since there is no tribunal, a heresy trial is decided in the scientific literature, normally through conducting research and publishing peer reviewed articles. Can you demonstrate that your heretical view is better than the current view? If so, it may become the new orthodoxy. Plate tectonics was once heresy in science but it's now orthodoxy.

While many would see what I'm saying as a criticism of theology, because it lacks the evidentiary structure and processes of science, I

---

23 Note that I think that is the wrong way to discuss prayer, but a huge proportion of the literature on prayer suggests things that *should* be testable. I discuss this further in Neufeld, Henry. Not Ashamed of the Gospel. Gonzalez, FL: Energion Publications, 2005, pages 35-54.

do not see this as a problem in itself. Theology is a different field from science, deals with different topics and thus has different methods and standards.

There are those scientists who see scientific study and the scientific method as the be all and end all of all knowledge. If they cannot demonstrate something scientifically, they will reject it.. But science is very good at describing, cataloging, and depicting what is. It is much less interested in what should be or what might be.

Sometimes scientists step across that line, and depending on how flexible they are at dealing with a different field, their results vary wildly. If they try to apply purely scientific reasoning to "should" questions, the rough edges definitely show.

Theologians, on the other hand, regularly get stuck with describing what is, or what they *think* is, and lose out to science on that score every time. Most commonly this results from determining what ought to be from scripture or by derivation from theological premises, and then refusing to see that empirical testing falsifies their propositions.[24]

> *Theologians get in trouble when they decide how the physical world ought to work and force the scientific evidence to fit.*

As an example, take young earth creationism. Young earth creationism is the view that the entire history of this planet, and generally also the universe, began only about 6,000 years ago. (Some young earth creationists allow for up to 10,000 years.) This is based primarily on how they understand Genesis 1 and 2, and then the genealogies of Genesis 5 and 11.

Now the physical evidence of the earth itself is becoming clearer and clearer that the earth is very old. The scientific estimate of 4.5 billion years is becoming firmer and firmer. Multiple lines of evidence from

---

24 That is why I predict a bad end for intelligent design. The evidences of theological thinking are rampant in intelligent design theory, and theological thinking is not well suited to solving scientific problems.

multiple scientific disciplines confirm this estimate. But certain theologians (or scientists behaving as amateur theologians) believe that the earth *must be* 6,000 years old, so they will go to any lengths to prove that it *is* 6,000 years old.

I don't want to go too far afield into the controversy and creation and evolution, but I do need to talk about interpretation here. We have already talked about different ways in which God presents his revelation. There are also different ways in which that revelation is presented to us, which means that there are different kinds of literature in the Bible. (Don't trust me on this. Don't assume that because it should be that way, it is. Just check out your Bible and see some of these different types of literature.

We can examine our understanding of both the scriptural and the scientific evidence to come to a better understanding of both.

Thus we don't have to throw out the Bible because of this difference. Young earth creationists suggest that if we don't believe Genesis on the age of the earth, why believe the Bible about anything. But while there may be controversy about progressive or continuous revelation, there is little about whether our knowledge can progress. We have to ask what the message of the passage is, and what the means is of conveying that message.

We are presented with several options in a case like this. We can discard scripture because it is wrong. We can discard scientific evidence because it must be wrong based on scripture. Alternatively we can examine our understanding of both the scriptural and the scientific evidence to come to a better understanding of both.

Christian fundamentalists do not want us to reexamine our understanding of scripture, because they believe that is set in stone. Oddly enough, some of the scientists who believe that science can provide all knowledge don't want us to reexamine our understanding of scripture either, because if our understanding changes then we wiggle out from under their attacks on our faith.

We don't need to be afraid of such attacks. We simply need to honestly examine all aspects of God's revelation on an issue, whether that revelation comes from the rocks, fossils, and living creatures of the earth, from a spoken word, or a written word.

Stick to God's word, not your understanding of it. Your understanding can always improve!

Let's look at another example, the virgin birth and the resurrection. On these issues I'm really pretty orthodox. While I believe that God made a universe that could run on its own, I also believe that God likes to communicate with his creatures. Thus I reject miracles that simply interfere with the ordinary functioning of the universe. I *expect* physical regularity. There are two reasons for this. First and foremost, I simply observe that the universe operates overwhelmingly in accordance with natural law. Such exceptions as may be claimed are few and far between. Even if I allow every miracle claim I've heard, it would only represent a minor ripple in terms of the operation of just this solar system, not to mention the universe. Second, however, even in religious tradition, story telling, and myth making, the actual impact of divine action on the world is kept distinctly limited. Because miraculous events stand out, we tend to overemphasize their impact. It is quite rare for religious literature to claim that divine action is truly replacing the day to day activities of the natural world.

The doctrines of the resurrection and the virgin birth state that God is fundamentally interested in communion with human beings.

There is, however, a deeper claim that's involved in both the virgin birth and the resurrection. These doctrines state that God is fundamentally interested in communion with human beings. In the virgin birth we have the statement that God is prepared to share our form and our condition and to become a part of that history. In the crucifixion, God says that he is prepared to carry that sharing all the way, to experience death. In the resurrection, he states that despite his willingness to share it, he's above it, and thus able not just to commiserate with us, but to redeem us. To those non-Christians who comment that the death of Jesus is not really a sacrifice because he knew he would be brought back to life, let me simply comment that from the Christian perspective, his sacrifice was equal *at least* to any of our physical deaths precisely because he also promised that we could return to life. According to Christian doctrine, nobody's death has to be permanent. Jesus came back to earth after his resurrection, but that was not for his benefit, but for ours. He had nothing to gain by popping in and out for a period of time.

We can easily affirm all of the physical facts of the resurrection and virgin birth and nonetheless miss the greater point of God's interest in and participation with humanity.

Now to maintain the unchanging nature of truth, we tend to focus on the physical facts of the resurrection. We maintain that Jesus truly died, that he truly was in the grave, and that he was miraculously and bodily brought back to life. Some people have problems affirming those things, though I do not, even though I cannot really test and prove them. At the same time, we can easily affirm all of those things and nonetheless miss the greater point of God's interest in and participation with humanity. And if we really think about it, I think we have to acknowledge that what the virgin birth and the resurrection expresses is more mind-boggling, and truly more difficult to accept than the physical events involved.

After all someone can believe that Jesus was divine by virtue of adoption by the Spirit at his baptism. Others believe that Jesus was raised, though not in a physical body, but a spiritual one. Others believe that the resurrection was somehow a spiritual event itself, in which Jesus would enter a different type of existence, if it can be called existence. In all of those positions one can still assert God's interest in us mortal creatures on this tiny planet, an interest he was willing to carry through 100%.

This means that the one mind-boggling Christian claim—that infinite God was willing to experience life as a finite creature, remains throughout. That claim is the one that is hard for me to believe. Having accepted that God could want such a thing, it is not hard at all for me to believe he could achieve it.

The concept of heresy thus becomes a problem for religion, in a way that it does not for science. The broad use of the term "heresy" to mean some kind of deviation from a defined orthodoxy tends to prevent us from following our speculations on physical miracles through to the spiritual reality behind them. It can prevent us from being in fellowship with someone who is one or two degrees farther down the line on a particular doctrine. The broader definition of heresy, which is commonly used in conversation, is "deviation from the (unchanging) truths of Christianity," which truths are generally defined by the speaker. But however defined, that view tells us that we nailed the absolute truth at some time in the past, and are never going to have an opportunity to review it, and that we must be prevented from doing so.

Theology itself also has a history of overturned positions.

I simply don't believe we can afford that level of certainty in theology. Theology itself also has a history of overturned positions. I think many of these overturned positions were in error, and should have been overturned. In other words, I don't see that God's truth has changed—just our conception of it.

People once believed that the sun orbited the earth, and based this belief on the Bible. While some claim this was a misinterpretation of the Bible, I think it was quite correct. The cosmology of the Bible is not distinguishable from that of the other ancient near eastern cultures, and the earth was flat and round, like a dinner plate, and the sun passed under it at night and over it during the day. The problem was not that people misinterpreted the Bible, it was that they applied the Bible in a way that was inappropriate. It seems arrogant to say that they applied it in a way God never intended, but that's how I see it.

People once used the Bible to support slavery. Many see that as a misinterpretation. But the Bible permits slavery, attempts to regulate it, but never outlaws it. I think it is morally wrong to hold slaves today, but this is based on working out principles into modern lives in ways that were never actually presented in scripture.

Currently we have struggles over the scientific role, if any, of the creation stories in the Bible. What do they tell us? Can we be certain?

It is incredibly dangerous to take something that is not universal, that is not timeless and treat it as though it actually is.

I think that the Bible really does say that the earth was created in a literal week. I suspect that those who first read those stories took that quite literally. Those who read it in that way today are not *stupid*. They simply hold a different view than I do of the *role* of scripture in knowledge.

God may not be bound by time, but we are, and thus when unbound divinity communicates with bound humanity, the communication is itself bound by time. It relates to the time, place, circumstances, and the participants in the act of communication. It is incredibly dangerous to take something that is *not* universal, that is *not* timeless and treat it as though it actually *is*.

It is my view that God continues to speak, sometimes in the very fabric of the universe, and sometimes in human minds. If we can't follow along with the continuing conversation, religious people will become irrelevant. On the other hand if we continue to search for the best in our past and combine it with the best of our present, we will be able to give sound (for the moment!) answers to the "should" questions of our lives.

Unchanging truth is perceived by changing people. Giving up false perceptions is not a denial of truth, but an affirmation of it.

SEARCH FOR AUTHORITY

I really cannot cover this subject solely as an examination of the role of the Bible as a written message, because this must be combined with both epistemology and with the notion of any divine message transmitted to any human at any time.

For many centuries, the only form of revelation which the community of faith claimed was actually oral, rather than written. Modes by which divine communications were thought to be received included the casting of lots, the Urim and the Thummim carried by the High Priest, or speech offered directly by a prophet under the immediate moving of the spirit of God. Did these methods of communication differ greatly in reliability compared with modern Bible study?

It certainly seems that in many cases, the word of the prophets was quite uncertain. 1 Kings 22 contains an incident in which various prophets were giving different messages, and indeed, the writer of the story appears to hold that God is the source of the lying messages as well as of the true ones, however indirectly (1 Kings 22:19-23). The true prophet, Micaiah, only tells the truth when he is forced to swear to do so. Then he prophesies Ahab's destruction. In this case, God

One man is said here to carry the message from God, whereas another 400 carry a false message.

is presented as lying through the prophets (or moving the prophets indirectly to lie) in order to bring about the destruction of Ahab, a king who was in opposition to His worship. Ezekiel 14:9 presents a similar problem.

The situation in 1 Kings 22 presented, in addition, the problem of determining who was actually the true prophet. One man is said here to carry the message from God, whereas another 400 carry a false message. I believe this problem relates closely to the modern problem of acceptance of particular literature as inspired and the problem of canonization. (I treat canonization, and inspiration of a book as two separate problems.) It is common to approach the problem of who is a true prophet through the test given in Deuteronomy 18:22, "When a word spoken by a prophet in the name of the LORD is not fulfilled and does not come true, it is not a word spoken by the LORD. The prophet has spoken presumptuously; have no fear of him." This test is a test for things which have already happened. It is a judicial test for dealing with someone who claims to speak for the Lord. It is not a test which is of value when one is listening to the prophet. In the case of Ahab and Jehoshaphat, they each had to make their decision before they would be able to apply the test of Deuteronomy 18:22. There is a second test for a prophet given in the book of Deuteronomy:

> *Should a prophet or a pedlar of dreams appear among you and offer you a sign or a portent, and call on you to go after other gods whom you have not known and to worship them, even if the sign or portent should come true do not heed the words of that prophet or dreamer." — Deuteronomy 13:1-3a (REB)*

There is a test of the prophet which can be done at the time of the prophecy. In this case there is a test of the prophet which can be done at the time of the prophecy. If the prophet asks you to follow *gods you have not known* then you are not to follow him. The experience of the hearer is related to the experience of the prophet so that the individual hearer can determine who speaks for God. Indeed, the test of Deuteronomy 18:22 is not universally applied. In the story of Jonah, by simply observing the test of fulfillment, one would have to consider Jonah a false prophet.

I think it is never the case that the term "Word of God" as used by Bible writers can properly be taken to refer to the Bible as Christians now have it, and it is only rarely the case that this phrase can be taken to mean such portions of written scripture as were available at the time. The prophet brings God's word for the intended audience at the time. No prophet, of course, would claim to actually contain God's word. It is the Word which creates (Psalm 33:6-9), surely not a function of a written book, or even of the words spoken by the mouth of a prophet. Thus, in applying the Biblical texts which relate to the "Word of God" to the written scripture we can get a very skewed idea of what the Bible writers meant by that phrase. One should also be continually aware of what would have constituted written scripture at the time of writing.

To understand properly the role which scripture should play in the life of a person of faith, it is necessary to first look at our basic epistemology, then the place of divine revelation as a whole, and finally to narrow this concept to that portion of divine revelation and how it is presented in scripture. Epistemology is the study of how we know things, how we determine what is true and what is false. People make these determinations in very different ways. Often the most bitter arguments occur because we misunderstand what someone else thinks is evidence, what is trustworthy, or what can be known.

Often the most bitter arguments occur because we misunderstand what someone else thinks is evidence, what is trustworthy, or what can be known.

First, we look at epistemology. This is a seriously neglected branch of study. Everyone who believes that he or she knows something will have some basis for that belief. Often arguments occur simply because two people are approaching their knowledge sources differently. For example, a person who believes that the earth was created in six literal days, and is absolutely certain of this fact, may debate with someone who believes the earth is quite old and that one species has developed from another through the operation of evolution. Upon pointing out any flaw in the theory of evolution, the creationist will think that he has won the debate because, while his view is monolithic and unflawed, that of the evolutionist has a weakness. He may, in fact, be very surprised that his opponent doesn't simply bow out. Why? Because to him, the fact that Genesis 1, read literally, refers to six days as the time during which the creation of the universe took place, means that this is a fact. No further evidence is really necessary to his way of thinking. Any one flaw in the theory of evolution will be sufficient to prove that it is much less believable. On the other hand, the supporter of evolution is likely to be quite shocked at this notion, since he sees no evidence at all (since he doesn't count the literal reading of Genesis 1 in the category of evidence) that the creationist's argument is true. This difference in epistemology will generally prevent constructive debate. An earlier question must be resolved first, namely, "What is evidence and what is not?"

Most people, even the most religious or spiritual, accept the results of modern science as it impinges on their daily life. Though I cannot go into great detail on the subject of epistemology here, I must summarize a few points. First, most people, even the most religious or spiritual, accept the results of modern science as it impinges on their daily life. Thus, they are willing to believe, or even to know, that their vehicles will function, that airplanes will fly, or even that their physician can prescribe an appropriate medication. These things are accepted as facts by the average person, and I think all but a few of the very religious. Can we know things for certain based on our reason and on application of appropriate methodology, the scientific method being the primary case in point? If we wish to obtain absolutely true information, the proverbial TRUTH, then we cannot do this. We are always operating on the basis of theoretical constructs, even when those constructs are very reliable and have been tested again and again. An electronics engineer can design a circuit with full confidence, despite the fact that one cannot be certain, in an absolute sense, that atomic theory is the true explanation of how electricity functions. Within our current ability to observe and test, we know of no case which these laws do not explain, but that doesn't mean we won't find one.

My point here is that these methods do not provide absolute knowledge, and indeed cannot provide it, but that we nonetheless live with this uncertainty on a regular basis. The arrogance of the suggestion that we possess absolute truth is something we must give up. What we possess is our best approximation of the truth within our current and individual limitations. (Note that while electricity works both for the electronics engineer and for me, my own understanding of the processes involved is considerably less accurate.) We thus do not possess absolute knowledge in the physical realm. We possess working knowledge.

Realization of this point for some people results in their believing that in the spiritual realm they can have that absolute certainty which they lack in the physical realm. This is an interesting view if for no other reason than that there are multiple claimants to the status of divine revelation. These include individual intuition, revelations directly from god(s), various written scriptures, including the Bible, the Qur'an, and the Book of Mormon, and the statements of particular religious authority figures. Out of this morass of supposedly divine revelations, how does one come to this absolute truth? I submit that one cannot, and that coming to believe that one can is a great destructive force in one's life, both intellectually and spiritually. What I am working towards is a functional knowledge in spiritual matters, not an absolute knowledge.

What I am working towards is a functional knowledge in spiritual matters, not an absolute knowledge.

There are some additional considerations about spiritual knowledge, in that, when we speak of God as transcendent, we must understand that we cannot understand that which transcends our own experience. What we *can* understand is what we actually experience. We then postulate what it might be "out there" that causes that experience. The tangible portion of Christian experience for the individual is that which he experiences for himself. For the world, it is the community of faith which is the objective evidence. Paul says, "Now you are Christ's body." (1 Corinthians 12:27). What can be objectively seen about the Christian religion is what can be observed about its members now and in the past. Often we'd rather people didn't see this, but this is, in fact, the only objective evidence for them to look at.

It is not the objective value of the scriptures themselves, but the validity of the experience they reflect which counts. And if that experience was only something which happened back then, then it will not ring true now. It only matters if the past experience was authentic and acted with power in the lives of the believers if the same power is present within the community now. I don't think the Christian church has done well in reflecting this fact. In terms of our understanding and doctrines about God, however, we must have a great humility, along with Paul.

Once we step outside of the "real" universe as we know it, and start speaking of eternity, timelessness, infinity, omnipotence, omnipresence and omniscience we are beyond our own capability to comprehend or catalog.

Once we step outside of the "real" universe as we know it, and start speaking of eternity, timelessness, infinity, omnipotence, omnipresence and omniscience we are beyond our own capability to comprehend or catalog. It's no surprise to me that the Apostle Paul in 1 Corinthians 13:9 said, "we know partially." If one has any idea of what one is talking about when one says the word "infinite" one should take "partial knowledge" as a given. Less than infinite mental capacity makes for less than full knowledge of something or someone who is, in fact, infinite.

For example, the logic of the "uncaused cause" escapes me—in a purely natural universe. It appears that one is saying, "My premise is true, therefore my premise is false." That is, "Since everything must have a cause, there must be an ultimate cause which is itself uncaused." This is a natural problem of trying to carry the logic of the universe outside its bounds, if it is proper to speak of the bounds of a universe as we do in theological discussions.

The uncaused cause argument does, however, demonstrate that we have to go outside of our normal natural logic when we deal with ultimate origins. We know of nothing that exists of itself, yet we know that things exist, thus there must be something that is outside the realm of physical experience, and not subject to physical experimentation, namely something that is self-existent. This doesn't prove that God exists, but it points to a philosophical niche where God will fit.

"God is infinite" is actually an easy statement to make, because it has no meaning to the human mind.

How could we then be said to experience the infinite? I contend that we don't. We experience something which seems less but is actually much harder to deal with. I would say that the message of scripture, especially in the Psalms is that God is adequate, that He is sufficiently powerful to accomplish what is needed, sufficiently knowledgeable to know what is needed and sufficiently present to be there when needed. "God is infinite" is actually an easy statement to make, because it has no meaning to the human mind. It essentially means "Someone-beyond-our-understanding is something-we-don't-comprehend."

This is not to argue that God is not infinite, but rather than we cannot comprehend infinity, so that it is more important to understand how we experience God than to play with phrases which try to describe an actuality which is beyond us. I have tried statements such as "God is infinite"; "God is omnipotent"; "God is omniscient" or even "God is good" on various audiences and found that few people are terribly certain what these statements mean.

I pray that you may have the power to comprehend, with all the saints, what is the breadth and length and height and depth, and to know the love of Christ that surpasses knowledge, so that you may be filled with all the fulness of God. — Ephesians 3:18-19 (NRSV)

That which cannot be known cognitively is nonetheless experienced personally. We need to perceive this directly. For too many people the scriptures become the sole way in which they can approach God, or to know him. The scriptures become a block between their perceptions and God, rather than a source of illumination. I illustrate this as follows:

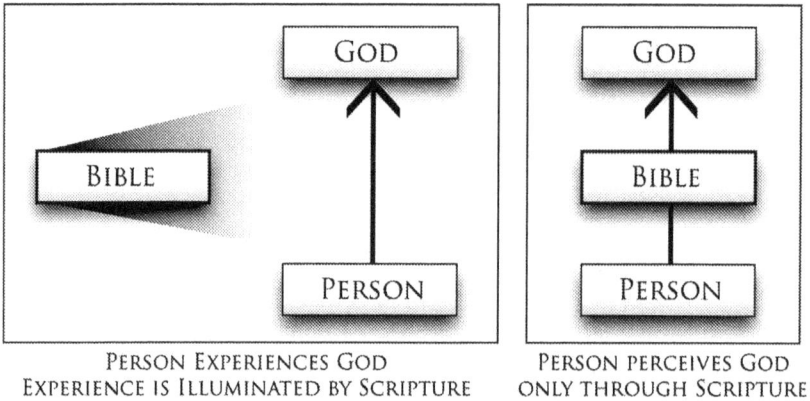

PERSON EXPERIENCES GOD
EXPERIENCE IS ILLUMINATED BY SCRIPTURE

PERSON PERCEIVES GOD
ONLY THROUGH SCRIPTURE

At a more basic level, I think this is precisely the kind of problem John is addressing in 1 John 4:20 (TNIV). ". . . For if we do not love a fellow believer, whom we have seen, we cannot love God, whom we have not seen.." Apart from this concept, the statement "I love God" is simply a version of "I place a value on someone-beyond-my-understanding." Most common, everyday Christians are well ahead of the theologians on this one. Look at Psalm 78. Here we have the illustration of the greater miracle, and therefore the less comprehensible and personal, not guaranteeing belief in the lesser miracle. Psalm 78:19-25 discusses the refusal to believe God could provide food following the rescue from Egypt and the passage of the Sea of Reeds. The experiential statement from this story is that one miraculous event does not necessarily cause trust for a future event.

BIBLE WRITERS AND AUTHORITY

Moses, Isaiah, Jeremiah, Ezekiel, Jesus of Nazareth —all of these people who have contributed words to what we call the Bible were innovators. They were unafraid to challenge what people around them thought. They were not slow to reinterpret the traditions they had received in order to present things in a new light, to adapt old laws to new situations.

Real Christians would be a dynamic force in society because they would really be presenting a way of life to the world.

Who are the heirs of the literature they produced, either as the fount in the case of Jesus, or as actual writers in the other cases? Can they be people whose best response to a new situation is to say, "My Bible says," when most of them haven't the faintest idea what it actually does say? Are the traditionalists, the "Bible believers," the heirs of Ezekiel ("This proverb will no longer be said in Israel", Ezekiel 18), Jeremiah ("I will make a new covenant" Jeremiah 31) or Jesus ("You have heard that it was said in old times . . . but I say unto you" Matthew 5)? Real Christians would be a dynamic force in society because they would really be presenting a way of life to the world. "Today I offer you the choice of life and good, or death and evil." Deuteronomy 30:15. We call on people to make a choice, but if they don't want to accept the Bible as inerrant, or infallible, or whatever it is we try to make them accept it as, we are unable to show why this way is any better than theirs. Why is this? Because Christians are in fact living no better, accomplishing no more than their non-Christian counterparts.

We don't exemplify the message of Deuteronomy 30:15. And we haven't the intellectual equipment or the training to explain why our moral values are actually better in any case.

So wherein lies the authority of the Biblical writers? Is there such a thing as authority in scripture?

THREE ANALYSES OF INSPIRATION

Let me approach a study of inspired writings from three different angles. These are by category of literature, by the process which produces the canonized work, and by communications model.

Categories of Literature

We have few words attributed to God, but we have many events attributed to him.

Let's first divide the literature of the Bible into categories and look at the type of material presented and the claims which are made for it. (This list is not intended to be detailed or exhaustive.)

Narrative or History

We have a considerable amount of narrative in the scriptures. This narrative is usually claimed as historical, though on occasion it is presented as a story which is told by one of the characters. In the narrative portions of the Bible we do not have a claim that God is speaking, but we have a description of what the writer believes God has done and an expression of the meaning of this action to the people of the writer's time. For example in the books of Kings Israel is presented as prospering when they worship the Lord and failing when they fail to follow him. The events of Israel's history, seen as actions of God with respect to his people, are presented with a particular meaning. We have few words attributed to God, but we have many events attributed to him. The claim of revelation in this type of literature is one of God's actions in history as observed by people. It appears clear that the author of

Kings is not claiming that his story is directly revealed by God, as he references the chronicles of the kings of Judah or of Israel as a source for all the deeds of various kings. Probably he is collecting history from those chronicles and presenting it with a particular "spin."

We might chart this as follows:

GOD ACTS ————————————→ HISTORY

WRITER OBSERVES, WRITES, AND INTERPRETS

Interpretation is a serious part of any story writing or telling. Let's take, for example, a modern story about a person who is shot in their home during a robbery. The person who commits the crime is carrying a handgun purchased legally. The victim is unarmed. A gun control advocate might tell this story with the lesson being that, were there just *Interpretation* tighter laws controlling guns, the criminal might *is a serious* not have been in possession of the weapon. This *part of any* version of the story would emphasize that the *story writing* criminal had a legally purchased weapon. It might *or telling.* also emphasize the difficulty of committing the crime with a knife, or with no weapon at all. Another person, an advocate of self-defense training and of gun possession for self defense might tell the same story with the emphasis on the weakness, lack of training and lack of defense of the crime victim. The conclusion in this case might be that if only the victim had been armed and perhaps trained in self-defense, he would today be alive. The events remain the same but the story is different.

Parables are especially subject to this type of interpretation. If we look at the parable of the unjust steward, we see a number of potential endings or morals drawn from the story (Luke 16:1-18). (Note that some would question whether all the sayings given in verses 9-18 were actually related to the parable in the oral tradition. But it appears that Luke finds them relevant.

Songs, Prayers and Poetry

Second, we have a number of songs, poems and prayers presented in connection with certain events. Again, these don't purport to be the words of God, indeed, they claim directly to be the words of men, often presented to God. Exodus 15 and Judges 5 are examples of such literature. Does anyone really believe that God celebrates the treacherous murder of a guest (Judges 5:24-27)?

In this type of literature, people respond to what they perceive as God's action, or to the actions of men which causes them to call upon God. We might chart it as follows:

EVENTS IMPACT ⟶ PERSON

WRITER OBSERVES, REPORTS, AND INTERPRETS

Fictional Writing

Fictional writing attempts to create a scene or scenario, or bring out some aspects of personality by telling a narrative which is not necessarily historically true. Included in this type of writing in the Bible are the parables of Jesus, the parable of the trees (Judges 9), and some would say the books of Ruth, Jonah and Job. It is certain that at least part of the book of Job is fictional, in that one doubts anyone was around recording these lengthy speeches in fine poetry, or in fact that such speeches would be given in conversation with a man in terrible pain. Each of these teaches a lesson or lessons through the narrative just as much as if it were narrating a true story.

The chart would be as follows:

IDEA OR ATTITUDE

$$\downarrow$$

PROPHET/WRITER, ACTS AS CREATIVE INSTRUMENT IN PRESENTING STORY

Each of these general categories of literature has a different approach used in its creation, and the same things cannot be said with regard to inspiration in all cases. Can Psalm 137:8,9 ("Happy is he who repays you for what you did to us! Happy is he who seizes your babes and dashes them against a rock.") be compared in inspiration to Leviticus 19:18 ("Never seek revenge or cherish a grudge towards your kinsfolk; you must love your neighbour as yourself. I am the LORD") ? (Both verses from the REB.)

Stages of Production

Another way in which we can divide the notion of inspiration is by stages in the production of what we later consider to be scripture. It is rare that a writer originally sets out to write scripture. When Paul wrote letters to churches, he was not trying to create the Bible, he was trying to respond to situations in the Christian communities of which he was often the founder. When Jeremiah is told to write his messages in a scroll, the purpose is clearly stated: "Perhaps the house of Judah will be warned of all the disaster I am planning to inflict on them, and everyone will abandon his evil conduct; then I shall forgive their wrongdoing and their sin" (Jeremiah 36:3, REB). There is no sense here of writing scripture which is applicable for all time. We are actually spectators in a process which has everything to do with the moment at which the message is presented. Neither Jeremiah nor

Paul are speaking directly to us; each is addressing a particular situation in his individual community at a particular time.

Following this addressing of a specific situation, the community recognizes the value of what the prophet or other writer has done, and collects, preserves and transmits the message. This may involve writing an initially oral tradition, as is likely in the gospel accounts about Jesus, or writing under the dictation of the prophet, as in the case of Jeremiah. It may involve editing several existing traditions as appears to have happened in the case of the Pentateuch.

With the material collected, it is copied and transmitted. It is hard for us to realize the immense difficulty involved in this, because we live in an age when printing is easy, and in fact electronic transmission is rather trivial. I intend to post this particular essay on my web page and e-mail it to a number of people. For others I will print copies on a laser printer. I will be able to do in a few moments what would take many hours or days of effort for somebody in ancient times. Each copy had to be made by hand. The potential for errors is enormous. I can't help but be awed by the preservation of scriptural texts considering the difficulties involved.

I can't help but be awed by the preservation of scriptural texts considering the difficulties involved.

Various materials which are accepted by the community of faith as somehow authoritative or useful in worship and determination of doctrine are then collected together, and we call the entire collection the Bible or scripture. This is known as the process of canonization. Canonization is somewhat misunderstood. Being included in the canon does not make a writing somehow more inspired than it was before. It is a recognition by the community of faith that a writing is inspired, and that its inspiration extends beyond the limitations of the time and place in which it was written.

The community interprets the writings, creating a tradition of interpretation. Many people do not realize the extent to which our individual experience and the experience of our faith community impacts the way we understand certain writings. One need only compare a Jewish view, a Christian view and a historical-critical view of the servant passages in Isaiah, which include the much cited Isaiah 53 to see how much a different perspective will change the way one reads a particular passage.

Very often our doctrinal views color our perception of scripture rather than the reverse. A common question I hear in Bible classes upon presenting an interpretation is: "But how does that fit in with the doctrine of _____?" The concern is not whether we are reading this particular author in context and understanding what he has to say, but how the passage relates to a creed.

As individuals, we interpret and apply the scriptures to our lives. It is this part of the process which can cause a great deal of difficulty. We each apply our own experience to our own understanding. We need also to apply the experience of others, and a view of objective reality.

Communications Model

We can understand a process of communication as involving a communicator, or speaker, a message and a listener. I will limit this discussion to getting a single message from one person to the next, without regard to responses. We can illustrate this process as follows:

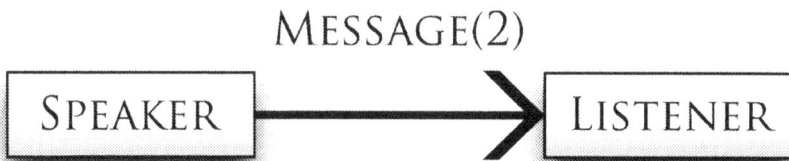

MESSAGE(2)

SPEAKER ⟶ LISTENER

When we speak about a writing which is divinely inspired, we add significant complexity into this picture. At a minimum we will have:

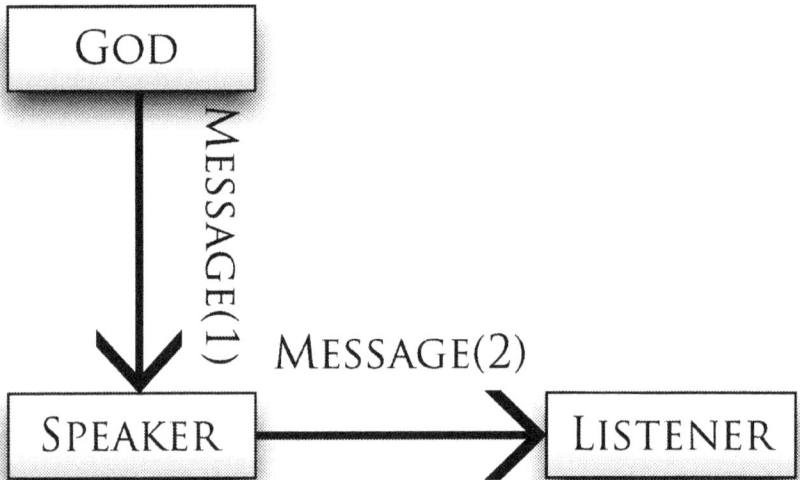

God provides a message by whatever means to a prophet who then speaks the message to a listening audience. I distinguish message(1) from message(2) because there is no fundamental reason to assume that the message received by the prophet is the same as the message spoken by the prophet. For this, further proof would be needed.

In the case of canonized scripture, however, we add additional factors into the pattern:

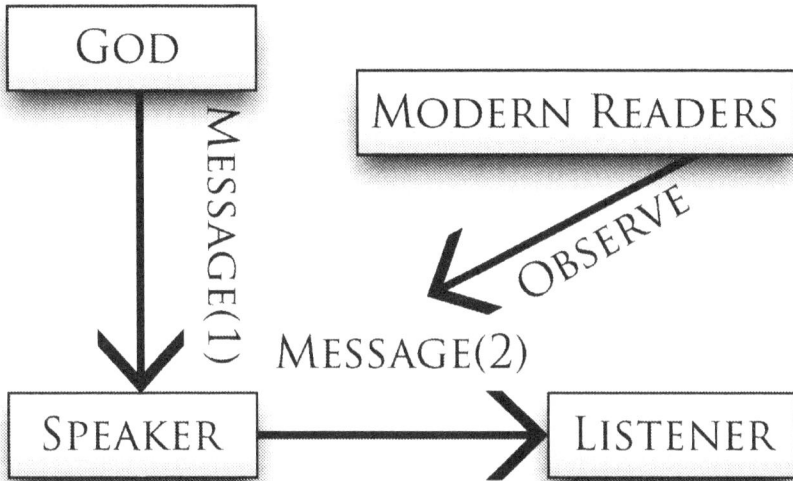

In this case, if we assume we have a message from God, that message is passed to the prophet, who passes it to his audience. We observe the message as it passes between the prophet and the audience.

Now there are a number of possibilities in terms of how this process can be viewed.

1. God [dictates to] -> Prophet -> Scripture [Scripture = Words of God; Prophet and audience have no effect]

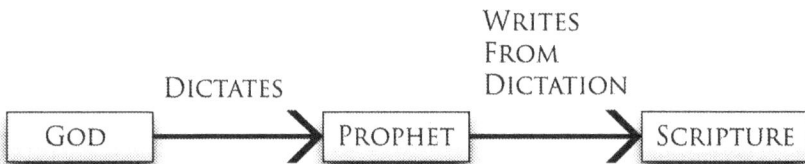

2. God [inspires and directs] -> Prophet -> Scripture [Words are protected; Prophet determines form but not meaning, audience is of negligible effect]

3. God [inspires and directs] -> Prophet -> Message -> Audience
[Both prophet and audience determine the form, but not the
message. This is typical of the standard view of inerrancy among lay
persons.]

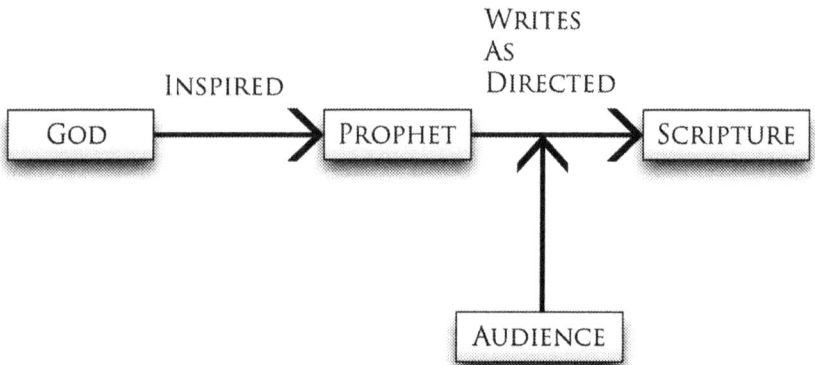

4. God [inspires] -> Prophet -> Message -> Audience [Both prophet
and audience condition the contents which are directed to that
audience, overall message is protected. Note that for some people
this is compatible with inerrancy as described in the Chicago
Statement, though most lay members find this a little loose.]

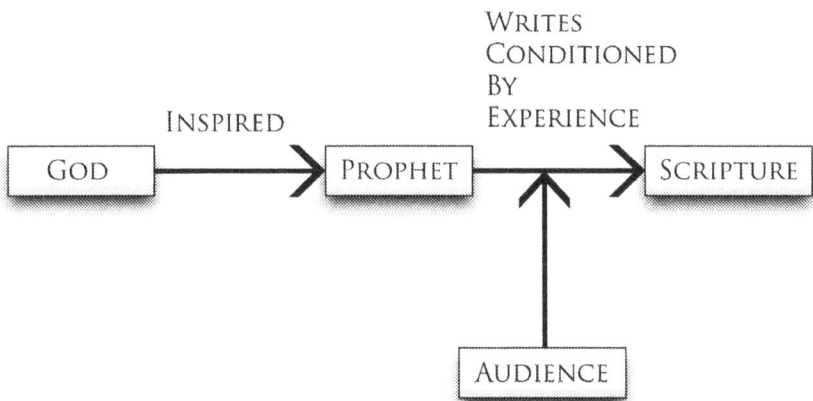

5. God [inspires] -> Prophet -> Message -> Audience [Both prophet and audience condition the contents which are directed to that audience, message is in human hands after the inspiration]

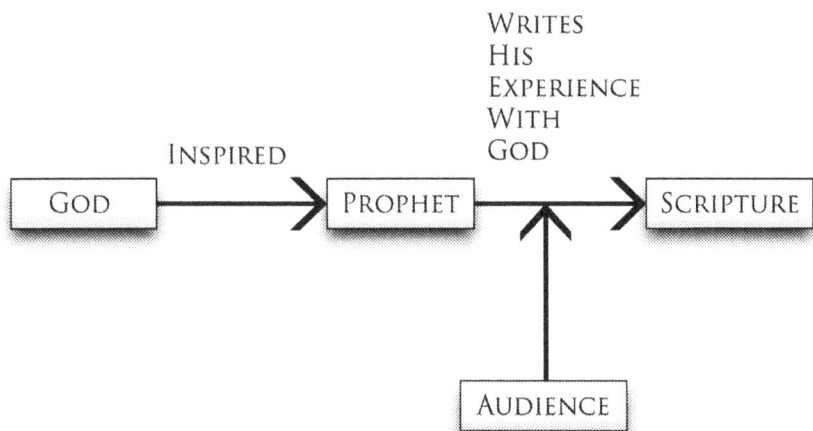

6. Prophet [feeling inspired] -> Message ->Audience [Inspiration consists in how much the reader agrees with the feeling of the prophet, in other words does the reader feel inspired as he reads?]

WRITES
HIS
EXPERIENCE

```
┌─────────────┐                    ┌──────────────┐
│  PROPHET    │────────────▶       │  SCRIPTURE   │
└─────────────┘       ▲            └──────────────┘
                      │
                      │
              ┌───────────────┐
              │   AUDIENCE    │
              └───────────────┘
```

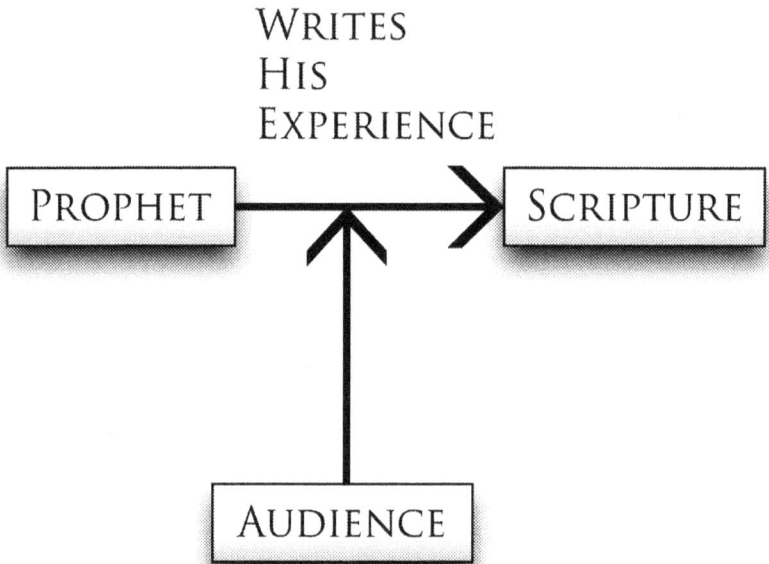

The first three forms do not give adequate place to the audience and the prophet. If the prophet is simply a tool, why does God make use of one? Why not simply speak? On the other hand, the sixth, and to a lesser extent the fifth tend to leave God out of the picture. Now one can understand why an atheist or agnostic would leave God out of the picture, seeing as he or she does not believe in God. On the other hand, it seems very unlikely that anyone doesn't believe that the audience exists. By the very fact of reading or perceiving the message the audience will place its own interpretation on the message.

Without further evidence to indicate otherwise, I would suggest that the prophet also leaves his or her mark on the message, as the widely varying styles of writing and even attitudes in the scriptures make very clear. It is only by ignoring the individual characteristics of the individual books or compositions which comprise the Bible that we can imagine that the whole was somehow dictated by God. The stamp of individual personality and of the time is all over the material.

TESTING AND AUTHORITY

WHAT IS AUTHORITY?

What God has said isn't only alive and active! It is sharper than any double-edged sword. — Hebrews 4:12 (CEV)

Everything in the Scriptures is God's Word. All of it is useful for teaching and helping people and for correcting them and showing them how to live. The Scriptures train God's servants to do all kinds of good deeds. - 2 Timothy 3:16, 17 (CEV)

We test the Scriptures by placing our trust in God and seeing what He will do for us through Jesus Christ.

The key word in this passage is "useful." Scripture should be a present guide to life and should be useful in our daily lives and in the life of the church.

The Law of the Lord is a lamp, and its teachings shine brightly. - Proverbs 6:23 (CEV)

TESTING THE SCRIPTURES

We test the Scriptures by placing our trust in God and seeing what He will do for us through Jesus Christ. "Discover for yourself that the LORD is kind. Come to him for protection, and you will be glad." (Psalm 34:8) "But if we live in the light, as God does, we share in life with each other. And the blood of his Son Jesus washes all our sins away." (1 John 1:7)

We place our trust in God, His Word and His promises, not in a book. God will fulfill those promises and validate His word in our lives.

> *Our LORD, you are true to your promises, and your word is like silver heated seven times in a fiery furnace. - Psalm 12:6 (CEV)*

ANSWERING QUESTIONS

Suppose you are using a hammer successfully to pound in a nail and someone comes by and starts pointing out the flaws in the hammer. They tell you it doesn't look very good, and perhaps it isn't too efficient. If it is accomplishing the task for which you bought it, what will you do? You'll keep on using it, of course!

All scripture is useful. - 2 Timothy 3:16 (CEV)

Though the Bible contains much history, we don't read it because we are curious about the historical details it contains. We read it to receive a message from God. If the Bible sheds light on our paths, then it is doing what it is supposed to do. Many people study and debate about errors and contradictions in the Bible. It takes considerable knowledge to enter that debate-knowledge of history, of languages, of interpretation, and of science. But there is one test we can perform, no matter what skill we have. We can apply the promises of God and verify them in our own lives.

> *You can tell what they are by what they do. No one picks grapes or figs from thornbushes. A good tree produces good fruit, and a bad tree produces bad fruit. - Matthew 7:16-17 (CEV)*

A Summary of Biblical Authority

The following is adapted from the Participatory Study Series Pamphlet *The Authority of the Bible*[25] and serves simply as a summary of the material presented thus far in this chapter.

The Bible and God's Word

The Bible is just one of the ways that God has to give us His word. The Bible contains God's word and conveys God's word and is God's word, but it is not all of God's word.

- God's word created the heavens and the earth (Psalm 33:6-9)
- God's word is shown in the heavens (Psalm 19:1)
- God's word comes through the Holy Spirit (John 14:7)
- God's word can come through the gift of prophecy (Romans 12:6)
- God's word can come through words of knowledge or wisdom (1 Corinthians 12:8)

Experience and Inspiration

We are basing our lives on experience that works. But this is not just our own experience. It is the experience of God's people through the ages as recorded in the Bible and in church history. It is not just our experience, but the experience of our fellow-believers.

Long ago in many ways and at many times God's prophets spoke his message to our ancestors. But now at last, God sent his Son to bring his message to us. God created the universe by his Son, and everything will someday belong to the Son. God's Son has all the brightness of God's own glory and is like him in every way. By his own mighty word, he holds the universe together. - Hebrews 1:1-3 (CEV)

Hebrews 11 describes many of these people of faith and then concludes: "All of them pleased God because of their faith! But still

---

25 http://participatorystudyseries.com/pss_full_pamphlet.php?sku=PSS007.

they died without being given what had been promised. This was because God had something better in store for us" (Hebrews 11:39-40a,CEV)

Many see the Bible primarily or even exclusively as a source of doctrinal information. In many cases they extend this to historical and scientific information as well. The Bible's value consists in the information one can extract from it. But the Bible isn't even primarily designed to give doctrinal information. It is a book of experience. "These things happened to them as a warning to us. All this was written in the Scriptures to teach us who live in these last days" (1 Corinthians 10:11, CEV).

God's word, brought to us in these various ways, also aids us in doing much more than just gaining information. It can:

The Bible needs to be understood as part of a community of faith.

- Help us resist sin (Psalm 119:11)
- Help us discern right and wrong (Hebrews 4:12, 13)
- Guide us in knowing what God will do soon (Revelation 1:1)

If the Bible is a valid guide, why do so many people understand it differently?

The Bible needs to be understood as part of a community of faith. "But you need to realize that no one alone can understand any of the prophecies in the Scriptures. The prophets did not think these things up on their own, but they were guided by the Spirit of God" (2 Peter 1:20-21, CEV)

We need the Holy Spirit and our brothers and sisters to help us understand God's message for us.

Your word is a lamp that gives light wherever I walk. - Psalm 119:105 (CEV)

Looking at Testing

Basics

We are instructed to test the spirits to see whether they are of God. In Deuteronomy 18:21-22 we are told that if God says something will happen, then it will happen. This is a way to test the word of a prophet. But we must modify this test with the words of Jeremiah (Jeremiah 18) and the example of Jonah in which the predicted event does not take place. But it does not take place for a reason-because the word accomplished its goal of correction.

Deuteronomy 13:1-5 provides another test that is easier to apply. If the prophet tells us to worship other gods, his message is not true.

This test can be applied before one waits for the fulfillment of any prediction. It even applies to prophecies that do not contain predictions.

We have talked a great deal about inspiration in this book, but let's look at it from the other direction. When you are confronted by a message that someone claims is from God, what do you do? I'm going to discuss the tests of a prophet, which might be equated to tests for inspiration, *There is no test for inspiration that is community independent.* that are used in Christianity. These find their source somewhere in the Bible.

These tests are derived from the community. In other words, they have their source in tradition. Tradition can be valuable, and it can also be a problem. Here the key element of tradition is that it reflects the approach of a particular community.

There is no test for inspiration that is community independent. In order to test whether a message is from God or not, one has to first determine just what it is that God would want to communicate. The common 20th and 21st century assumption is that God wants to communicate information. This is an age of information.

But why do we assume that, other than that we are obsessed with information? In fact, this determination that God will provide information and will do so in a particular format is simply another example of making God in our image. We want data, so a good guide will supply us with data.

Since the ultimate standard must be God, by what standard then can we judge just what it is that God communicates? The test, I believe, operates at the level of the community. For us as Christians this begins back when Abraham heard God's call and accepted God's blessing (Genesis 12).

The promise made to Abraham, seen as an act of grace received by faith, is the starting point of God's revelation and of God's salvific activity.

Why do I not say something like Adam, Enoch, or Noah? Because Abraham is the one that got the process of revelation started. It was Abraham's descendants, whether spiritual or physical, who provide the remaining revelation. Other revelation is then tested against that original revelation.

I believe this point is inherent in Paul's use of the Abraham stories in Galatians:

> [15] *Brothers and sisters, I give an example from daily life: once a person's will has been ratified, no one adds to it or annuls it.* [16] *Now the promises were made to Abraham and to his offspring; it does not say, "And to offsprings," as of many; but it says, "And to your offspring," that is, to one person, who is Christ.* [17] *My point is this: the law, which came four hundred thirty years later, does not annul a covenant previously ratified by God, so as to nullify the promise.* [18] *For if the inheritance comes from the law, it no longer comes from the promise; but God*

granted it to Abraham through the promise. —
Galatians 3:15-18 (NRSV)

There are numerous exegetical issues in this passage, but here I simply want to note that the promise made to Abraham, seen as an act of grace received by faith, is the starting point of God's revelation and of God's salvific activity. The two are intertwined and founded in the same event.

From this event comes the community, first of Judaism, and then of its descendant Christianity. That is the foundation of the tests of inspiration that I will present.

The tests I'll be discussing in the next few pages are:

- Fulfilled prediction or sign
- Godliness
- Access to inside information, or is in God's councils
- Divine wisdom
- Gift of discernment

The Bible does make allowances for predictions that are true, but not from God.

All of these have been claimed to be good methods of deciding who is a true or false prophet.

FULFILLED PREDICTION

Let's look first at the fulfilled prediction or sign. The basic scripture for this particular test comes from Deuteronomy 18:21-22, which says that if a prophet says that something is going to happen, and then that doesn't happen, they are a false prophet. Note that this is not stated positively, that is one cannot be certain simply because a prediction comes true that the person making that prediction is a true prophet. We'll discuss that further in the entry on "Godliness" as a test.

This seems to be the easiest test as well as the most objective. We simply look for some external sign, normally a predicted event, and if that does not occur as predicted by the prophet, then we know the prophet is false. But the Bible does make allowances for predictions that are true, but not from God, and we ourselves know that there is a possibility of a prediction being true simply by chance, or because someone knows certain factors and gets lucky. For example, one can look at opinion polls and predict the result of an election. That doesn't make that person a prophet.

The book of Jeremiah provides many excellent examples of the use of this test. The primary issue between Jeremiah and other prophets was over the status of Jerusalem and the temple. Many prophets were predicting that the city and temple would be saved. They held a doctrine that based on God's promises to David, the temple could not be destroyed. Jeremiah predicted that Jerusalem and the temple would be destroyed and the rulers and many of the people taken into exile. History proved Jeremiah right, even if his behavior during an invasion did sound like treason.

Revelation has gone through many interpretations that have been proven false by the progress of history.

One more specific example was the conflict between Hananiah and Jeremiah in depicted in Jeremiah 28. Jeremiah uses the visual aid of a yoke that he wears to show that those who accept Babylon's yoke will survive. Hananiah removes the yoke and prophecies that Nebuchadnezzar will be repulsed. Jeremiah then predicts Hananiah's death as a punishment from God. In the same year Hananiah dies (Jeremiah 28).

A further problem with this test is the vagueness of certain prophecies. People frequently object when I refer to Biblical prophecies being vague. Usually these people have a very precise interpretation in mind. But there are normally other people who are equally convinced of precisely opposite solutions. A good example is the white horse its rider of Revelation 6:2. Interpretations, strongly stated, include the contradictory positions that the rider is Jesus

Christ himself, and that he is the Antichrist. Some other interpreters see the early Christian church heading out to evangelize. Obviously not all of these can be true, and so the prophecy must be regarded as vague. Revelation has gone through many interpretations that have been proven false by the progress of history. Remaining interpretations put unfulfilled events in the future. Can one then know by the fulfillment/sign test whether John the Revelator was a true or false prophet?

But the situation gets more complicated yet. In the book of Jonah we have the story of a prophet who makes a specific prediction, one that certainly cannot be regarded as vague, and does not admit of an alternate interpretation. Nineveh was to be destroyed in 40 days. Nineveh was not destroyed in 40 days. One cannot assume that the later destruction of Nineveh fulfilled this prophecy, because it did not occur within the 40 days (Jonah 3:4). Failed prediction! Can we say to the Ninevites, "You don't have to fear Jonah's prediction (Deuteronomy 18:22)?" That is certainly not the position of the book. From the perspective of our story teller Jonah does, in fact, have a message from God, but nothing happens.

Jonah does, in fact, have a message from God, but nothing happens.

Some will claim that Jonah is a fictional story written to make a different point. I would argue that whether fictional or not, it likely reflects its author's view of predictive prophecy. But we have a better alternative.

Returning to Jeremiah, now to chapter 18, we have the story of Jeremiah in the potter's house. He watches the clay pots being made, and sees the potter reshape clay into whatever form he likes. This is often used by Christians, following the example of Paul in Romans 9, to indicate God's absolute sovereignty, apart from our own actions. But Jeremiah's point is precisely the opposite. He is telling us that God can change his actions based on repentance. Read the entire chapter. When good is predicted, and people turn to evil, God will repent of the good he had planned to do. When evil is predicted, and the people repent, then God will repent of the evil. The entire chapter is very instructive, and basically carries the same message with reference to prophecy as the book of Jonah.

The historical situation in Jeremiah is substantially different from that in Jonah, however. Jeremiah is responding to the doctrine I referred to above, that Jerusalem and the Temple could not be destroyed because of God's promises to David. Jeremiah is responding to this that God can change his actions according to the decisions and actions of people. In Jeremiah's case this resulted in his correct prediction that Judah would fall, and would go into exile. He also predicted their return to Judah with significant accuracy. Jeremiah essentially presented a doctrine that, despite Deuteronomy 18, would allow the earlier prophets, those who had brought messages in favor of Jerusalem and the temple, could be true prophets even though their prediction of an eternal throne for David and for Jerusalem's prosperity were about to fail.

I call this the "dead test" for a prophet, because you're so very often dead, as were many inhabitants of Jerusalem, before you can finish applying the test.

The final difficulty with this test is simply that the results can be too late. Again let me use Jeremiah for an example. He predicts the destruction of Jerusalem. The majority of those who claimed to be prophets in Judah were predicting salvation for Jerusalem. If you were Jehoiakim, Jehoiachin, or Zedekiah, who would you believe? Until the events have taken place, you cannot know whose prediction came to pass. I call this the "dead test" for a prophet, because you're so very often dead, as were many inhabitants of Jerusalem, before you can finish applying the test.

So this test has some value, in that it provides an objective test, but at the same time there are substantial difficulties in application.

GODLINESS

The second test in my list is "godliness," but this is just a shorthand name for the test as proposed in Deuteronomy 13:1-5.

> *If prophets or those who divine by dreams appear among you and promise you omens or portents, [2] and the omens or the portents declared by them take place, and they say, "Let us follow other gods" (whom you have not known) "and let us serve them," [3] you must not heed the words of those prophets or those who divine by dreams; for the L*ORD* your God is testing you, to know whether you indeed love the L*ORD* your God with all your heart and soul. [4] The L*ORD* your God you shall follow, him alone you shall fear, his commandments you shall keep, his voice you shall obey, him you shall serve, and to him you shall hold fast. [5] But those prophets or those who divine by dreams shall be put to death for having spoken treason against the L*ORD* your God—who brought you out of the land of Egypt and redeemed you from the house of slavery —to turn you from the way in which the L*ORD* your God commanded you to walk. So you shall purge the evil from your midst. — Deuteronomy 13:1-5 (NRSV)*

What you expect a scripture to accomplish for you generally comes from your background.

What this passage proposes is that a person could arise who claimed to be a prophet, and who could actually produce a sign, or make a prediction that would be accurate, and yet that person would advice the Israelites to worship gods other than YHWH. Despite the fulfillment of the prediction, that person should be regarded as a false prophet.

This is essentially a version of what I proposed as the fundamental source of what a person regards as scripture when I discussed community and scripture. It may annoy people who believe they have the very best scriptures in their religion to think that the major reason one accepts a particular scripture is the community in which one grew up. (Note that I do not claim this is universal–just very common.) What you expect a scripture to accomplish for you generally comes from your background. So the essential question, especially for written scripture, is how good the community is at finding and identifying scripture.

In our Deuteronomy passage this is formalized into a test. If the prophet is leading you astray from your existing faith, then that prophet is not a true prophet. This argues for coherence in a community's scripture, normally a fairly obvious need, and it provides some sort of rudder for where the stream of revelation goes for a particular group.

Each of these tests has its strengths and weaknesses.

Again, this test is not complete. Some of the positive aspects include:

- It does not require you to wait for the fulfillment. You can know immediately if someone is off track.
- It helps keep the community spiritual tradition unified.
- Under many circumstances it provides a clear answer.
- It acknowledges the possibility of true predictions from someone who is not speaking for God.

But on the negative side:

- It does not provide any objective answer; the community simply identifies the prophet with what it already accepts
- It is inherently conservative; a prophet bringing new light will often appear to be challenging the fundamentals of the community
- It tends to put spiritual revelation in the hand of theologians.

Each of these tests has its strengths and weaknesses, which is why we have so many different ones.

Divine Wisdom and Discernment

Now let's look at the last two items on my list, divine wisdom, and the gift of discernment, which are closely related.

As a preliminary, let me comment that I have noticed that most of the gifts of the Spirit have their "talent" counterparts. There are those who exhibit wisdom, and then there is the gift of messages (or words) of wisdom. There are talented teachers, and then there are those whose ability to help guide a group into understanding spiritual truths seems supernatural. There is a talent for languages, and then there is the gift of tongues as exhibited on Pentecost with everyone hearing in their own language. I believe such a relationship between a wise person, and one who has the gift of discernment or shares in the divine wisdom.

Wisdom writers, on the other hand, appeal to the nature of the created universe, to the experience of how God works, and to the understanding the community has built up.

I'm combining my discussion, because I think the relationship between wisdom exhibited as wisdom (a Proverbs sort of wisdom) and the gift of discernment is very close. I think we ignore that relationship at our own peril. The problem is that the gift of discernment doesn't have some specific physical manifestation to identify it. It can be claimed in the same way as the gift of prophecy, or as any message from God. One person can make the claim of the gift of prophecy, while another claims discernment and backs them up. The result is just as circular as any other test I've mentioned.

So let me start with wisdom. I think it is critically important that we pay attention to the fact that the Bible includes wisdom literature. Many of the Psalms, and the books of Proverbs and Ecclesiastes fall into this category. If you pay attention as you read these books, you will see something significantly different from the message of the prophetic books. The prophets stand on their claim to receive messages from God through the Spirit. Their sanction is their inspiration by God. They invite you to accept or reject their message, and experience the consequences (graphically presented) of your choice.

Wisdom writers, on the other hand, appeal to the nature of the created universe, to the experience of how God works, and to the understanding the community has built up. They are clear that the message comes from God and is a divine message, but it is a process of the mind that has perceived God's revelation. I don't believe that this is any less "inspiration" than the prophet's message, but it invites the reader to participate in another way, by thinking and getting themselves involved in the divine wisdom.

People grow in wisdom by looking into God's actions, in the physical, spiritual, and moral realms.

Jesus also spoke in this wisdom mode. There has been a debate amongst historical Jesus scholars about whether Jesus was a wisdom teacher or an eschatological preacher, with the latter being similar to the prophetic approach. I would suggest that the question narrows Jesus too much. Jesus spoke in the form of wisdom at times and in the form of prophecy (Spirit driven speech) at times. One of the reasons I think that those on the outside couldn't understand the parables was that the parables were not in the form of announcements; rather, they were in the form of seeds. It's wrong to look for **the** interpretation of a parable. One needs to look for how a parable can seed into one's thinking and change one's whole approach to life. That is divine wisdom operating within.

But divine wisdom is not a purely human endeavor. It is not that people figure out God. Rather, it is that people grow in wisdom by looking into God's actions, in the physical, spiritual, and moral realms. Psalm 119:104 says we get wisdom through God's precepts.

Sometimes I add this to my list of tests–the obedience test. If we set out to obey God with all our hearts and minds, we will not ultimately be led astray. When we are led astray, it's because in some sense we have kept an agenda other than finding divine wisdom. Wisdom literature emphasizes that wisdom starts with fearing God (Proverbs 1:7). Following God's wisdom involves acknowledging him as creator, and finding his wisdom in the creation (Proverbs 8:22ff, Psalm 104). Divine wisdom is one thing that appears to be promised on the only condition that we seek it wholeheartedly (James 1:5).

That divine wisdom forms the foundation for our understanding of discernment in the community. I think by now anyone who has stuck with me through all these essays will realize that I put the greatest weight on the community of faith in discerning God's message. Abraham had very little community to work with. We're told in Joshua 24:2 that Abraham's family were worshiping other gods. He simply had to move on faith. God honored his determination to obey and gave him direction clearly enough. Over time, the community of faith has exercised its discernment in preserving and granting authority to certain written material as part of our body of faith literature. The study of canonization is itself fairly complex. Let me just say here that if we do not believe that God leads spiritually in the community as it selects a body of literature that is authoritative, we should probably give up the notion of any canon at all.

My lousy spiritual eyesight can be aided by many different views.

If we do accept God's working in the community, then the more times we have someone who has heard God's voice, the greater the body of knowledge we have to work from. I suspect that God expects more in terms of discernment from me than he did from Abraham on this issue. Not because I'm wiser than Abraham, or more spiritual, or anything of the sort, but because I have much, much more material to work with, and thus many more ways to check what I hear.

In sports that allow plays to be reviewed, the reviewer can see the play from various camera angles. Often I look at a play as it's shown on TV and I see one thing, and then some other camera angle makes it clear that the reality was somewhat different. Abraham had one camera angle. I have many. My lousy spiritual eyesight can be aided by many different views.

I would suggest that the gifts of wisdom and discernment relate very closely to the divine wisdom and need to be judged as such. A "word of wisdom" or as I prefer, "message of wisdom" is something that can be tested by the community at the time it is spoken. We especially compare it to the divine wisdom. Does this word reflect the fear of God? Does this wisdom reflect God's activity in the world? Is it in accordance with God's precepts from which we get understanding? An absolute statement by someone who claims discernment can be tested in the same way.

We need to make divine wisdom the hallmark of our community.

One final comment I need to make has to do with how we find an objective standard. Obviously I believe that the Bible is a valid source for me in terms of faith and practice. Otherwise I wouldn't belong to a denomination that claims that as a doctrine, and I wouldn't be a Bible teacher. I think, however, that our witness needs to be more community based. As Christians we need to make our witness clear. We cannot simply provide a list of reasons one should regard the Bible as true; we need to show that the Bible is the book of a community in which God is present. I think this is where we frequently fail. We frequently fail because while we've accepted some pronouncements as true (which is good), we have failed to let the divine wisdom be planted in our hearts and minds and start to bear fruit.

We need to make divine wisdom the hallmark of our community.

In the Divine Council and Conclave

The third of those items on my list of approaches to determining whether a message comes from God is "Access to inside information, or is in God's councils."

You may be wondering, and rightfully so, how I distinguish this from other approaches. Surely this one is totally covered by the prediction or sign test. But I found this specifically in the foreword by Mark Chironna to Jim Goll's recent book, *The Seer*, which my wife and I are studying together. The statement there was that ". . . the earmark of a true prophet was that they stood in the divine council and conclave."[26]

We can't just discuss the theology of how inspiration works and assume that people can apply that knowledge practically.

What struck me immediately is that this is the type of statement that is commonly made by either theologians or very spiritual people who are experienced in prayer and in dealing with issues regarding the prophetic. I don't really take exception to it except that "earmark" normally means something like "a distinguishing or identifying mark." I get regular questions from people who have received impressions, visions, dreams, or heard something that they believe was the voice of God. How are they going to know whether this is God's leading or not? If someone has claimed that God told them something, how does one know whether they truly are? This "earmark" is unlikely to work well, because the question remains of where the mark is. What does the inexperienced person do?

I have seen this kind of answer in conferences, and people appear satisfied with them, but I also know that when they go home they still have the same basic question—how can I know. In other words, the earmark doesn't work well, or isn't visible to most people. I'm going

---

26 Goll, Jim. <u>The Seer</u>. Shippensburg, PA: Destiny Image Publishers, 2005, p. 12.

to deal with this more as I proceed through this series. But right now I just want to suggest that the answer to a question like this has to be practical. We can't just discuss the theology of how inspiration works and assume that people can apply that knowledge practically. Very often I think that those who proclaim the theology don't themselves know how to apply their knowledge practically and then just play it by ear. That can be very dangerous if the issue is a question of whether someone is speaking for God.

Some also will simply claim that nobody now is speaking for God. But those Christians who claim that the gifts of the Holy Spirit have ceased still need to deal with the issue of Biblical inspiration itself. Anyone can still ask why one should accept the Bible as inspired, and not other works from ancient times. In addition, there are Christian groups who claim that prophets still speak in modern times. (Jim Goll, whose book I cited earlier, is one such.) So in any case, one needs to have some kind of practical approach to these problems.

There is no such thing as "taking the Bible" apart from an interpretive framework.

BEING A JUDGE OF SCRIPTURE

I believe I am accepting the Bible just as it is, and that the inerrancy approach imposes meaning on the Bible that is not there. I do not approach the Bible as I do because I lack the faith to believe God could inspire scriptures in any way he wants. I approach it that way because that is the Bible that we have.

There is no such thing as "taking the Bible as it is" despite the many people who claim to do that. Their claim is simply empty. There is no such thing as "taking the Bible" apart from an interpretive framework. I believe that such a framework can be consistent with what the Bible is, or it can be completely imposed from outside, but it always requires justification. No passage of scripture was addressed to me, personally, in a specific set of my circumstances. Thus every application requires me to interpret some Biblical passage in such a way as to discover God's guidance for me.

I believe this is possible. I don't believe it's easy. I believe the responsible thing to do is for each of us to admit that we are following our best understanding, but that it is our understanding.

APPLYING THE WORD

There's a substantial difference between discovering just what the Bible says in a particular passage and learning how to apply that knowledge in your own life. You may read, for example, that Ananias and Sapphira were struck dead when they didn't give the whole amount they had promised from the sale of a property to the church. But what does that mean to you?

Does it mean that if your tithe check at church next week is less than 10% of that week's income you will be stricken dead?

Does it mean that if your tithe check at church next week is less than 10% of that week's income you will be stricken dead? Probably not. If that were the case, there would either be many less people in church, or the collections would be much greater!

There are other options. It might have been an isolated incident. There might have been some specific thing in their lives that caused it, or it might have been an event appropriate to the early church, but not to a later time. The concern may not have been the money at all, but their attitude toward the Holy Spirit and their willingness to lie.

We call the process of figuring out how the scripture applies in your own life *application.*

APPLICATION

Application carries us back again to just how you can learn God's will for you in your particular situation. It's often not nearly as easy as it seems. Intelligent, honest people come to very different conclusions. Many churches, for example, refuse to allow women to serve in leadership positions (complementarianism), while *In the same way as we respond to different spoken messages from God and different interpretations, the final choice has to be made by you.* others allow all persons to serve, and even ordain women as pastors (egalitarianism). Both of these positions are held by conservative Christians. This is not merely a liberal versus conservative debate.

Where does this diversity come from? Well, it all comes from the Bible. Those who do not permit women to teach cite texts such as 1 Timothy 2:12, in which Paul says he doesn't permit women to teach or have authority over men, or 1 Corinthians 14:34 which is very similar. They can cite these texts and announce that they are following what the Bible obviously teaches, while everyone who disagrees simply doesn't care about the Bible.

Those who support positions of trust for women will point out women leaders such as Deborah (Judges 4 and 5) or a reference to Junia as an apostle (Romans 16:7). In support of this they also quote Galatians 3:28, that in Christ there is neither male nor female, and that Paul himself talks about women speaking in church in 1 Corinthians 11:3-16.

This is not a book on interpretation and application, so I am not going to disentangle all of these issues. Again we see that the largest differences in the way people understand the Bible appear in the way we make use of it.

In the same way as we respond to different spoken messages from God and different interpretations, the final choice has to be made by you. The scriptures do not replace your own mind guided by the Holy Spirit.

Before we go on, however, let's look at some approaches to interpretation and application and just what they might mean in practice.

Approaches to Interpretation

The following four approaches and their variants will probably cover most Christian interpretation.

1. **The proof text method.** In this approach we see the Bible as a set of dicta about how to live and act. In looking for guidance in a particular situation, we search for a text which provides a command for that particular situation. This method can run aground on complex, modern situations which are not directly addressed, and also on the appearance of disagreement between various proof texts. For example, if someone in my church offends me, should I handle it as Matthew 18:15-17 says, ending with ". . . treat him as you would a pagan or tax collector" or as the nearby Matthew 18:22 says by forgiving him 70 times seven? (Those who solve this using context or comparison are not using a pure proof text method.)

Many theological disputes are perpetuated in this manner precisely because, in the Biblical texts, two views are in a state of tension.

2. **Proof texts in context.** Even if we place these texts in context, what we often do is try to avoid what one or the other is saying. We give precedence to a certain text. Many theological disputes are perpetuated in this manner precisely because, in the Biblical texts, two views are in a state of tension.

When I was college age and working in a small Christian school with my sister, we had a dispute over how to deal with a group of kids if you were having trouble with one or just a few. Is it proper to punish the entire group by detaining them after class, or must you carefully pick out the perpetrators? Most Americans, being individualists, will argue for the latter. In the dispute with my sister, however, we both had perfectly good texts to fall back on. Exodus 20:5, ". . . punishing the children for the sins of the parents . . ." or Joshua 7 with the story of Achan's entire clan being stoned for the sin of one of them would tend to support the group response, whereas Ezekiel 18 which says "It is the person who sins that will die" (v 4) supports the individual response. Even if I carefully see each of these passages in their literary context, they appear to support different courses of action.

The point here is not which one of us was right, but rather to point out that we could each cite quite good scriptures in support of our respective positions.

The Bible can be seen as a collection of the experiences of the people of faith with God, and a record of the action of God in history.

3. **Principles.** This view involves extracting the principles behind various commands and trying to separate them from the cultural context. God is seen as communicating what he can within the limitations of the understanding of the people receiving the communication. In this case, we might suggest that the passages in Exodus and Joshua, cited above, come from a time when guilt was considered more collective, and the individual was seen as a part of his tribe and not as a separate entity. As the culture grows, with the Israelites under the pressure of the exile, a message is sent relating guilt and salvation to the individual. This would be necessitated by people observing who was and was not exiled. Is the entire nation suffering, including the good, for the actions of an evil leadership? Where is justice? This view is a variety of progressive revelation. The main difficulty with progressive revelation is that it is often difficult to identify the trajectory, to tell which way the revelation is going. For example, is seeing the tribe or

clan as collectively responsible for its behavior more or less advanced than seeing the individual alone as responsible?

4. **Experiences.** The Bible can be seen as a collection of the experiences of the people of faith with God, and a record of the action of God in history. We then look from our experience to the collective experience throughout the history of the people of God for authentication. In this view, which I am advocating in this book (with a number of caveats on the short statement given here) the Bible is not primarily a source of laws or doctrines but a source of continuity and authority in the experience of the community as a whole, and from that, for the individual. As an example of the difference in approach, I recall when I was first approached with questions about the Pensacola Outpouring (revival at Brownville Assembly of God in Pensacola FL). Immediately I called to mind 1 John 4:1, "My dear friends, do not trust every spirit, but test the spirits, whether they are from God; for there are many false prophets about in the world." But just how does one test the spirits? (Read the next few verses, though you many still wonder just how you do it.)

But there are many things that are Biblical in either a general sense or some specific sense that are not Biblical in our particular circumstances.

A common approach is to take the following requirement of acknowledging "that Jesus Christ has come in the flesh" as a kind of a doctrinal statement. To accomplish this, one would have to collect a list of the doctrines of those who speak at the revival and compare them against some kind of doctrinal list. I didn't and don't take it that way. I listened to the testimonies of those who had attended with one question in my mind: Have these people been brought into an authentic experience with Jesus? How do I determine authentic? By comparing the visible results of the experience with the historical experience of others in the community of the faith (Matthew 7:16). Are all the results right? No. Some people respond with pride and feel more righteous and holier than others, because they have been revived. (See Matthew 13:1-23 for the authenticity of an experience which also involves misunderstanding and misuse.)

FROM INTERPRETATION TO AUTHORITY

Interpretation does not automatically equal authority. It's easy to forget this because we are so used to assuming that if something is Biblical, it must also be right. But there are many things that are Biblical in either a general sense or some specific sense that are not Biblical in our particular circumstances.

This process attempts to first establish the authority, scriptures, and from there to derive a set of data from the authority, which then may lead to an experience.

An easy and obvious example is the command to Abraham to leave his homeland and go somewhere God would show him (Genesis 12:1). That is a command that was correct for Abraham. It carries principles of obedience that are correct for any time. But it is not authoritative for me right now. God doesn't want me to leave my house and my homeland today.

What we're looking for from God's word is direction and authority, and in order to be valuable, that authority must be applicable to our particular circumstances.

WHAT IS AUTHORITY?

A typical approach of Christians in presenting the gospel message is to attempt first to prove that the Bible is true and trustworthy, and then from there to lead a person to understand and affirm a set of doctrines about Jesus Christ. In this connection I consider statements such as "all people are sinners," "all people are in need of a savior," and "salvation is a free gift of God" to be essentially doctrinal statements as long as they are presented as affirmations of theological fact.

This process attempts to first establish the authority, scriptures, and from there to derive a set of data from the authority, which then may lead to an experience. But we establish the authority before the experience.

I believe that this approach to spiritual experience is backwards. We need to view the present, personal experience with God as the most important part of our message, and as the most important source of authority in a person's spiritual life.

I expect that you are beginning to think I am advocating an approach which is totally subjective, that what the person feels is by itself a standard. This is only partially true. Everything is seen through the experience of the individual mind. We can't get away from this. However, one can compare one's personal experience with the experience of others. In addition, wherever one's spiritual experience impinges on material reality, one can objectively check what has happened. For example, if the story of Peter walking on the water is true, then were one to find a time machine and go back to the time in question and watch, one would see Peter walking on the surface of the water. If Peter in fact sank, then one would find that a spiritual claim—I am empowered to walk on water—is not objectively true.

I believe truth is one, but I believe that no human mind is capable of totally comprehending it.

In addition if one's experience leads one into completely uncharted waters from the point of view of one's community, though this doesn't mean one is necessarily wrong, it may mean that one must ever more carefully check what one is doing.

God is the final authority. The individual is in connection with God and experiences God, growing out of the experience of the community as a whole. Not only are the scriptures important here, but all of the history of Israel and of the church. In addition, the knowledge of other sources with reference to religious experience are important because we cannot truly understand the experience we possess in a vacuum. We cannot afford to pretend that traditions other than our own don't exist. It is not an abandonment of one's own tradition to seek actively to understand the traditions of others. Be careful not to confuse this with being your own authority. You are the one who must make the final choice, but you do so according to God's standard.

Am I advocating relativism here? No. I am advocating first a humility concerning our knowledge of the truth, and second a serious and continuous search for expanded truth. I believe truth is one, but I believe that no human mind is capable of totally comprehending it. This means that each of us should remain humble. The existence of absolute truth does not mean that I can know it; admitting my limitations does not mean that I have abandoned the value of truth itself. Admitting that I will change if new evidence is found doesn't indicate a lack of confidence in my present experience; it means rather that I am open to new experience and new truth as it may be found.

There is truth and falsehood in all traditions (including my own) but that we must work to gain more truth and reject falsehood wherever we find it.

Is there truth to be found in traditions other than my own? Yes, I believe there is. It is common among Christians to believe that all other religious systems are perversions of the truth. I believe instead that there is truth and falsehood in all traditions (including my own) but that we must work to gain more truth and reject falsehood wherever we find it. I am personally convinced that Jesus of Nazareth perfectly represented God to the world and is the savior of the world (Hebrews 1:3 is especially pertinent), but this does not mean to me that only Christians have any true knowledge about God or that all other systems started with truth and perverted it. Romans 1 contradicts this, for example.

Sources of Authority

Drawing from my Methodist tradition, let me borrow the Wesleyan Quadrilateral in order to present my view of the sources of authority and how we understand and validate our religious experience.

The quadrilateral combines Scripture, experience, tradition, and reason in forming doctrine.

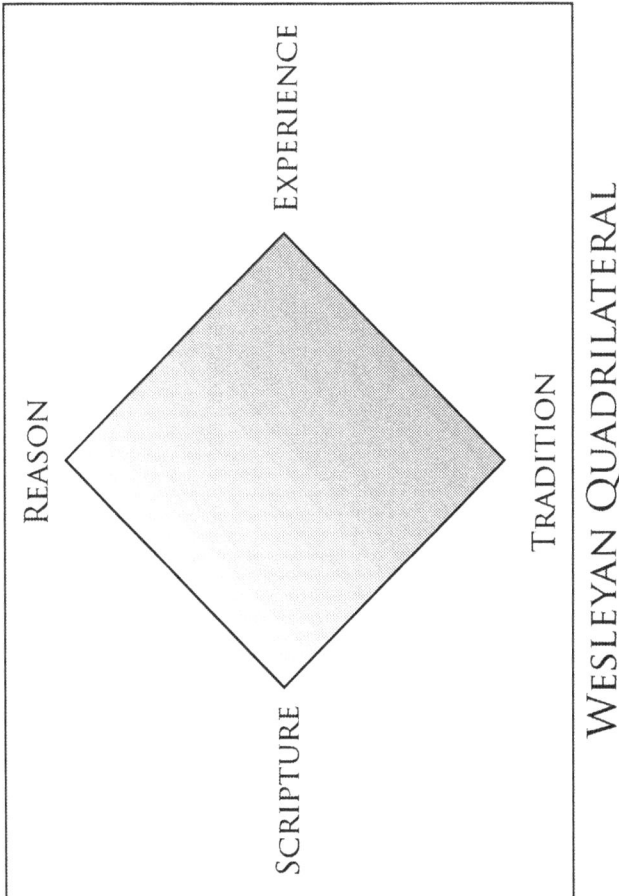

Many readers may object to placing the labels at the points rather than along the lines, but I prefer this representation because I don't believe one ever using any one of the elements by itself. My experience and my knowledge of Christian tradition changes the way I understand scripture, for example.

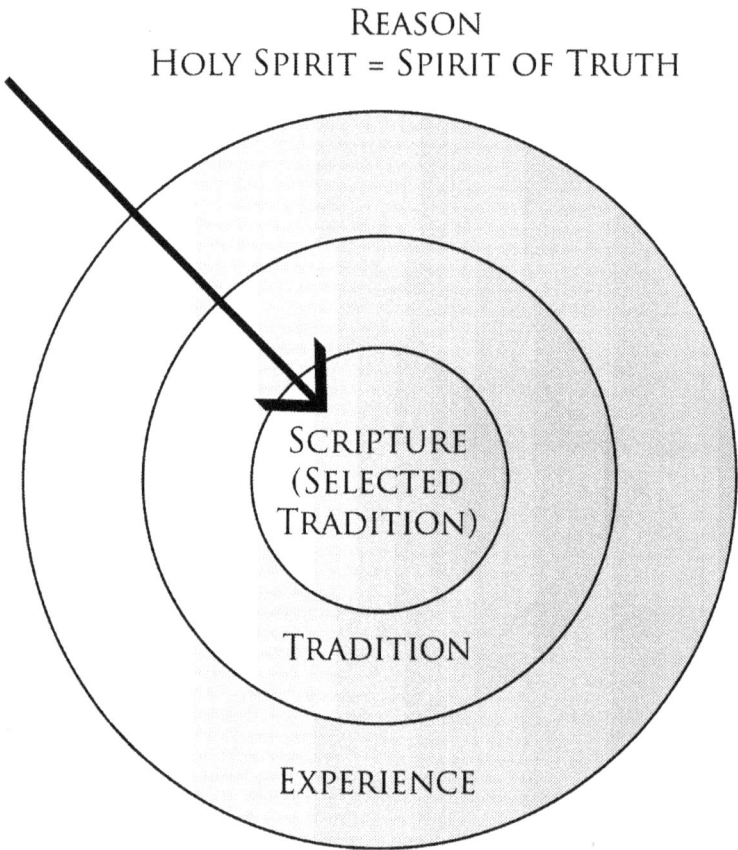

REASON
HOLY SPIRIT = SPIRIT OF TRUTH

SCRIPTURE
(SELECTED
TRADITION)

TRADITION

EXPERIENCE

In the figure above I represent the involvement of the Holy Spirit throughout this process.

188 - When People Speak for God

Scripture is the selected, authoritative core of our faith tradition. That is, we select from those things which God has revealed to us as a people the writings which are most important to us and which we hold in common. This selection we call canonization. Canonization, as I have said, is not a process of making something more inspired or holy, but rather is the recognition both of the inspiration of the work and of its abiding and general importance. A message could be very inspired, but only of importance to a small group of people or for a limited period of time. It would be no less holy in the sense of which I am speaking, but would nonetheless not share in the authority of the canonized writings.

What do I mean here by authority? Is this different from the authority above? No. It is only different in perspective. That is, in this case we are asking what joins our religious experience together as a community. That commonality is the canon of scripture. Our personal experiences differ seriously. Our traditions diverge at many points. John Wesley is very important to my tradition as a member of the United Methodist church, but he is not recognized as a source of authority or doctrine by Presbyterians. Presbyterians use Calvin as a source, but would not award the same value to Wesley as I do. Now neither tradition is asking for a place for either of these individuals in the canon of scripture, but they are part of each tradition, and they have an impact on how we understand tradition and scripture. Augustine is not recognized as scripture, but he is a part of the more general Christian tradition.

Without a present experience, and without the participation in the community of faith, I think the Bible is just another book.

I believe this works into a process somewhat as follows: We observe the core of our faith, and our scripture through the understanding and organization provided by our tradition. We understand our tradition in relation to our personal experience and we sort all of this via our reason. I believe that the concept of *sola scriptura*[27] or "the Bible alone" is not a reality. Even those who claim most to be following it are very much tied up in their creeds and in the tradition of their groups. I do not even think that *sola scriptura* is desirable. Without a present experience, and without the participation in the community of faith, I think the Bible is just another book. It is when we meet God in the Bible, and when we meet and become part of the community of faith through our common experience of God that the Bible becomes more than a bunch of words on paper.

Thus again, authority is in the divine and in the joining of the experience of the individual with that of the present and the historical community.

WHAT IS THE BIBLE?

It is the recounting of the things which God has done, of the actions of God in the history of the people of Israel which leads to the keeping of the commands

I believe that the Bible is a book of experience. I am often asked for a verse in the Bible from which I get this. It's not a verse as such, and I note that there is no verse which says that the Bible is a series statements of doctrine or theology either. (Note that 2 Timothy 3:16 in the KJV says that scripture is profitable for doctrine, not that it is doctrine. I believe that experience is more profitable for doctrine than any number of statements.)

A passage of scripture which I believe illustrates this approach is Psalm 78. In this teaching Psalm, the great acts of God in the history of Israel are recounted, and Israel is enjoined to keep them in mind.

> *"They were charged to put their trust in God,*
> *to hold his great acts ever in mind*
> *and to keep his commandments." (Psalm 78:7)*

---

27 I refer here to "sola scriptura" in the popular sense. As taught by Martin Luther and other advocates, the concept does include the way in which we are enlightened by other sources.

It is the recounting of the things which God has done, of the actions of God in the history of the people of Israel which leads to the keeping of the commands and to an understanding of the teaching. In Psalm 104, following the poetic description of the creation and the natural world, we have the statement:

> "Countless are the things you have made, LORD; by your wisdom you have made them all; the earth is full of your creatures." — Psalm 104:24 (REB)

This is followed by the response:

> "As long as I live I shall sing to the LORD; I shall sing psalms to my God all my life long." —Psalm 104:33 (REB)

The present experience is related to, and compared to the experience of the past, and also to the understanding of that experience.

And only then the following of the law, or the right action:

> "May my meditation be acceptable to him; I shall delight in the Lord. May sinners be banished from the earth and may the wicked be no more!" — Psalm 104:33-35 (REB)

This theme is so prevalent in scripture that we have the term "Heilsgeschichte" or "salvation-history" which is commonly used in studies of the theology of the Hebrew Scriptures especially. But this same theme is carried over into New Testament writings, especially in the Gospel of Matthew. Matthew goes to great pains to draw parallels to similar themes in the Hebrew scriptures and to root the understanding of Jesus in the community experience and understanding of the past. In many cases in which it is thought that Matthew is trying to claim a fulfilled predictive prophecy, he is actually pointing out such a parallel theme.

An example of this is Hosea 11:1 which is quoted in Matthew 2:15. If one reads the Hosea passage in context, it is clearly not a prediction at all, and in fact is an historical reference in the prophet's writing:

> *When   Israel   was   a   youth,   I   loved   him;*
> *out   of   Egypt   I   called   my   son;*
> *but the more I called, the farther they went from me;*
> *they   must   needs   sacrifice   to   the   baalim*
> *and   burn   offerings   to   images.   — Hosea   11:1-2*
> *(NASB95)*

To turn this into a prophecy would involve making some rather undesirable connections. Would we really care to apply "the more I called the further they went" to the life and ministry of Jesus? What Matthew is trying to do here, however, is parallel the idea of Jesus' ministry with the spiritual journey of Israel. This can then be followed by making a parallel of the liberation from sin provided by Jesus with the liberation from physical bondage provided by the exodus from Egypt. Thus, for Matthew, the present experience is related to, and compared to the experience of the past, and also to the understanding of that experience.

To slaves escaping from Egypt, I would imagine that the experience was not directly spiritual.

Let me clarify here the difference between an event and a theological understanding of that event. To slaves escaping from Egypt, I would imagine that the experience was not directly spiritual. They would not look at the deliverance in symbolic terms because there was a very real, physical meaning to the deliverance before them. The more symbolic and theological interpretation develops over time, in this case through the prophets and leading up to the understanding which came as the result of the exile. The exile could then be interpreted or understood in terms of the exodus experience. An example of this is found in Ezekiel 20.

Note that the impact of this type of experience is both ways. Not only do people come to understand their present experience (the exile and restoration, the ministry and death of Jesus, etc.) in terms of past experience, but they come to understand the past experience differently by reference to present experience. The Exodus had new meaning for the Israelites in exile and after their return. Christians will understand the exodus experience differently based on their understanding of the mission of Jesus.

This clarifies some very important things about a book of experience. First, the experience grows in the telling. This isn't a bad thing. As we collect experiences with God our understanding should grow. Many Christians are uncomfortable with this, thinking that the old understanding was wrong and therefore useless if a new understanding comes along. But experience is not like that. I have come to understand experiences I had as a child or youth in much different ways as I grew. This didn't *The* invalidate the experiences or the understanding that I *experience* had at the time. As a matter of fact, I can find great *grows in* value precisely in those experiences in which I was *the telling.* most wrong at the time. Second, the book of experience is not simply a narration of past events. It is rather a book of interpretation of those events and of an understanding of their meaning. And an event need not have just a single meaning. The facts and details of the event are not the most important part here. It is the growth of understanding of that experience in the community.

Notice where the doctrine comes in each case. Very little direct doctrine is taught in the Torah (the first five books of the Bible). We see both an experience of God and we see commands. One of the reasons I believe Christians find this portion of the Bible of little interest is that they are looking for neatly packaged observations about God. There are a few of those, but mostly there is an experience, interpreted, and then there are commands. I would relate these commands to "training in righteousness" as discussed in 2 Timothy 3:16. These commands shaped a people; they very literally made generations of experience. The Jewish people are what they are today because of how these laws have shaped their lives and their relationship to the world. If we do not look at what these laws accomplished in action we will not understand them. If we ignore them, or essentially dismiss them as a whole bunch of types pointing to Jesus as antitype, then we lose a major block of the experience of our community. And I do consider using these simply as types to be essentially a dismissal. What is the point of chapter after chapter of laws which simply point, not very clearly at that, to the Messiah and then have no further use? Christians need to deal constructively with this material in terms of how we understand our history if we wish to claim any sort of authentic Jewish heritage.

We then have the books of history, and only after that do we have the prophets and writings which take this experience

All must lead from experience to experience.

and make of it a more theological construct and begin to develop the great theological themes. The soaring poetry of Isaiah 40-66 is a major example of a near redefinition of the understanding of an experience, building it into serious theological themes. But even that is an interpretation built to deal with a particular experience, and we can look back at it now as another facet of the experience of the community of faith.

It is in this interpretation of the experience that we build doctrine. We cannot comprehend infinite God. We can only perceive Him as he is manifested in His creation. We should have a great deal of humility about our doctrines and about how we relate those doctrines to an ultimate reality. I like Tillich's phrase "ground of all being" for God, even though I don't agree with all of his theology. We can't claim to even understand all being; how much less can we claim to comprehend the basis of it all! Thus I would see doctrine as what leads us to an understanding of our own spiritual experience and allows us to communicate in a limited way our understanding of the creator. But all must lead from experience to experience. That which we can communicate in words is simply inadequate to describe the personal experience, and belief in a set of doctrines is nothing like a personal, spiritual experience.

Read the first chapter of Ezekiel quickly, concentrating on the struggle for words to describe what the prophet sees, or look in Revelation chapter one to see a struggle for words to express a vision. Any new Christian I know struggles for words to describe the personal experience which he or she has had. It is the long term Christians who have a font of words, but often those words sound hollow. If your experience, your goals, your pursuit of righteousness turns easily into words, perhaps you should examine that experience and see if it is still living.

I'm not necessarily speaking here of some kind of esoteric vision experience, the kind of "moment I met Jesus" experience which some can relate. For some people this is a very slow process. For some there is no conversion, because they began the path with their earliest memories, and each experience is only a further commitment to something which is already a part of them. I am talking about a living enthusiasm for doing what one knows to be right, for following truth wherever it may lead, for loving and caring for those one finds in need. A real, living experience will be a source of energy. Paul describes the gospel as the "power of God . . . beginning in faith and ending in faith." Unfortunately it seems that for many the experience is one of cutting themselves off from people, of making them feel superior and arrogant, as though the gospel gave one a corner on God.

I am talking about a living enthusiasm for doing what one knows to be right, for following truth wherever it may lead, for loving and caring for those one finds in need.

There may be some who are concerned that I am taking the objectivity away from their view of Christianity. Frankly I don't believe that the objectivity was ever there. A portion of our beliefs is objective. But we cannot prove past events, especially past miracles to the extent that they become proven or certain. It is when these events match an experience in our own minds that we attain belief. As the song says: "You ask me how I know He lives; He lives within my heart." Despite the metaphorical nature of the imagery (living within the heart) this expresses the personal experience. We find the answer in our experience and in our hearts and consciences (2 Corinthians 4:2b). Certainly there must be a basis for the experience, but the only reason we need an external kind of validation is if we wish to psychologically force our view and our understanding on someone else.

Faith ultimately must and will come through an experience of God's presence through his Holy Spirit.

I do not mean to imply here that we cannot discuss our faith or provide any evidence in support of the way we view the world. But I do believe that faith ultimately must and will come through an experience of God's presence through his Holy Spirit. Until that happens, nothing else will work. If that happens, nothing else is needed. The place for evidence is in clearing the way for that to happen. We do not need to demonstrate that God speaks through the Bible, nor do we need to demonstrate that God exists; we merely must show that it is not impossible for a rational person to believe in God.

If the way is clear, so that a person doesn't automatically reject any experience of the divine no matter what form it may come in, then God can speak, and that person can hear. It is quite possible, however, for someone to simply reject any possibility of God speaking in the first place, any possibility of a spiritual presence in the world, and such a person will have to explain any spiritual experience in some other way.

The comment in the parable of the rich man and Lazarus comes to mind. "And Abraham said, 'If they do not listen to Moses and the prophets they will pay no heed even if someone should rise from the dead.'" (Luke 16:31) I think part of the point here is that it's not about believing that someone rose from the dead, or even will rise from the dead, but about accepting an experience with God. Matters of life and death will follow on nicely after that experience. A genuine experience can function without a club to force others to agree.

I note that when the distinction between the saved and the lost is described in Matthew 25:31-46, it is not on the basis of what doctrines one believes, but on action. The point is made especially in verse 40: "And the king will answer, 'Truly I tell you: anything you did for one of my brothers here, however insignificant, you did for me'" (REB). Just as we can't describe our experience fully in words we can't judge another's experience (Matthew 7:1) but we can look at fruits (Matthew 7:16). I'm afraid it is in the last category that we, as Christians, fail the most often. Too often we are heard proclaiming a set of doctrines, but not a way of life, and to the extent we proclaim a way of life, we often fail to live it. The one objective test we are given, we fail.

Too often we are heard proclaiming a set of doctrines, but not a way of life.

I want to discuss briefly methods of interpretation, or how we get from this experience to an understanding of what the experience means in our own lives.

There is a distinct difference between historical study of the Bible and application of it to doctrine. Historical study should be as neutral and scientific as is possible. I approach this by use of the historical-critical method and I read material by people of a variety of belief systems in using this approach. Paul makes this statement: "An unspiritual person refuses what belongs to the Spirit of God; it is folly to him; he cannot grasp it, because it needs to be judged in the light of the Spirit" (1 Corinthians 2:14, REB) I believe that this verse has been used too often to justify intellectual laziness. If someone doesn't understand my interpretation of a particular passage, then I can accuse him or her of being unspiritual. If this were the case, how would anyone every become a Christian? They would have to somehow cross that barrier. I believe that the meaning in the context of a passage is plain enough, and that the best way to determine this historical meaning is through scientific study. What requires spiritual discernment, and indeed a spiritual experience is the application and comparison to an individual experience. But this is a separate issue from determining what a text actually says.

I'm not afraid of what might be found in historical study. I personally tend to be fairly conservative in my use of critical methodologies and my acceptance of the results. But acceptance of this type of study as a scientific endeavor is necessary, I believe, if we are to have any integrity in our understanding of what the experience of the Christian community actually is. Thus I don't describe those whose results are more liberal than my own as being under the influence of Satan (as *As far as I* I've heard it said), but rather simply as those who *can see* disagree with me on technical points. The argument *the Bible* here is methodology. We can disagree on spiritual *is almost* issues, and probably will, but this is a completely *totally* separate issue from historical study.

As far as I can see the Bible is almost totally unlike a boy scout manual.

BIBLICAL DECISION MAKING

In posting on my blog, Threads from Henry's Web,[28] I encountered the issue of slavery. Does the Bible condone or even encourage slavery? One answer is that it depends on the circumstances. Just how do we derive principles from scripture that can then be applied in the 21st century as Biblical truth?

The most common analogy I've encountered for the Bible is that it is like a boy scout manual. The problem is that as far as I can see the Bible is almost totally unlike a boy scout manual. If it were, we would be able to make Biblically based decisions simply by opening up the Bible, going to the handy index, and finding the instructions for what we are trying to do. Making a fire? Go to the right page, and you have the directions. Setting up a campsite? Different page, but still a clear answer.

---

28 http://www.energionpubs.com/wordpress.

The Bible is a book containing a large number of stories, and materials from a variety of documents, often ones written from a different perspective. By assuming the kind of unity that would be expected of a scout manual, we often miss what the Bible is actually saying. For example, which attitude toward foreigners is more appropriate, that of Jonah, in which God saves them even though that makes his prophet angry, or that of Nehemiah who runs all foreigners out?

I like the analogy of a toolkit, though this is only one of many. My basis for this starts with Proverbs 26:4-5: "[4]Do not answer fools according to their folly, or you will be a fool yourself. [5]Answer fools according to their folly, or they will be wise in their own eyes" (NRSV). OK, so which is it? Or should one continue to forgive over and over again (Matthew 18:22), or should one take the matter to one's congregation (Matthew 18:15-17)? It would depend on the specific circumstances. I know that I have often encountered cases in which a fool required answering (and what do I do about the command of Jesus not to call **anyone** a fool?), and many other cases in which the best choice was silence. I take the tool from my toolkit that seems to work best, and I hope I have wisdom to use the right one. The final decision about how you behave is up to you. It's up to you to choose the tool.

It's up to you to choose the tool.

Another common analogy is the the law code. Again, I have to ask whether people who use this analogy have actually read law codes. The Bible does contain law codes, but as a whole it is almost totally unlike a law code. With a law code, one again looks for the prescription for a particular topic and simply applies that prescription. But nobody actually keeps all the Biblical commands, especially those who are the loudest in claiming that they do. There are generally good reasons for this. For example, Christians do not keep the laws about animal sacrifices because we believe that the purpose for those laws has now passed. They have met their fulfillment in the sacrifice of Jesus.

Consider the recent ten commandments case in neighboring Alabama. The chief justice of the state supreme court placed a ten commandment monument in the courthouse. We had the odd image of Christians bowing down in front of the monument to the ten commandments (I know, they weren't worshiping it, they were praying *about* it), and protesting its removal. Removing the monument was supposed to be a major blow to moral values. But the vast majority of the people who were protesting do not keep the command written on that monument to keep the seventh day of the week as the Sabbath. I'm sure they have good reason to ignore or alter that command–I don't keep Saturday as the Sabbath either–but nonetheless isn't it interesting to place a monument to a command that most seem to agree was altered?

Why is one applicable and not the other? Or how many of those people do you suppose have pictures of Jesus on their walls at home or at church? Does the word "image" come to mind? Now I really have no problem with pictures of Jesus, other than that I've rarely seen one that has even a prayer of looking anything like the real thing, but certainly at least the Jewish interpretation of one of those commands forbids **all** images.

In the area of selective commands, what about Leviticus 18:22, "You will not lie with a man as with a woman." Now I've heard this one proclaimed many times with firm tones or pulpit pounding as appropriate. But I frequently then point these individuals to Leviticus 19:33-34, which says, "[33]When an alien resides with you in your land, you shall not oppress the alien. [34]The alien who resides with you shall be to you as the citizen among you; you shall love the alien as yourself, for you were aliens in the land of Egypt: I am the LORD your God" (NRSV). When I quote the second verse, I am always presented with plenty of reasons why this is not applicable in modern America, because the foreigners will overrun us and bankrupt the treasury when they all go on welfare. But why is one applicable and not the other?

You can probably produce reasons why one should be kept and the other not. But those reasons simply reinforce the point. We do not keep all the laws. We do not follow a simple process of looking for a prescription that matches our particular problem. We have to look for principles, and then make *choices* as to how we will behave.

I present these illustrations to show that generally those who claim to follow the Bible do, in fact, pick and choose according to circumstances. The difference is that I openly acknowledge that I do it, and I think it is the right way to do things. In fact I'm frightened by people who thing they can and should keep all the commands, because they might actually try to do it! In Deuteronomy 21:18-21, we have the instructions for arranging for one's rebellious son to be stoned. Is that applicable or not? Both the Jewish and the Christian traditions have dealt with such commands in such a way as to make them more humane, if they apply them at all.

When I do discover something powerful in the Bible it is much more likely to be a way to approach finding an answer than to be the actual answer.

Those Christians who are about to complain about my use of references from the Hebrew scriptures should consider Acts 5 and the story of Ananias and Sapphira. What is the appropriate penalty for lying on your pledge card to your church?

The best approach is to look at all the tools available, and make the best choice for my particular circumstances. This means that in many cases tools may come from something other than scripture. The Bible provides me with input, but it is not the only source of input that I have. In each case, I have to consider the source of my material, and its cultural background. But the key to my approach in the Bible is that I use the scriptures more to teach me about listening to God and how to recognize God's voice than I do to discover specific answers. When I do discover something powerful in the Bible it is much more likely to be a way to approach *finding* an answer than to be the actual answer.

I think that if you can discover where God is headed in a passage, that will be a good principle to work from, but it is often very hard to discover that principle. So how can we tell if we're getting it right?

As a Christian I have a simple answer for this. I start with Jesus. Jesus is my example. His command is to love one another as he has loved us (John 15:12). Jesus tells us a bit more about this principle when he talks about the two laws.

Jesus said that all the law and prophets could hang on two laws—love God and love your neighbor—so when you have an application of scripture, try to hang it from those two laws.

34 When the Pharisees heard that he had silenced the Sadducees, they gathered together, 35 and one of them, a lawyer, asked him a question to test him. 36 "Teacher, which commandment in the law is the greatest?" 37 He said to him, " 'You shall love the Lord your God with all your heart, and with all your soul, and with all your mind.' 38 This is the greatest and first commandment. 39 And a second is like it: 'You shall love your neighbor as yourself.' 40 On these two commandments hang all the law and the prophets. — Matthew 22:34-40 (NRSV)

I call this the hanging principle. Jesus said that all the law and prophets could hang on two laws—love God and love your neighbor— so when you have an application of scripture, try to hang it from those two laws. If your application of a scripture won't hang there, or looks out of place, perhaps you should look elsewhere. Those two laws are widely attested in scripture and in tradition. Because the

Bible contains both the ideal and the real, that approach keeps one looking to the ideal.

But the bottom line is that I simply don't expect the Bible to make my decisions for me. In other words, I don't expect to find a specific command for my time and circumstances. I have to make decisions and live with the consequences. One thing that I can see happening in the Bible, in the scriptures of many other faiths, and in a broad range of human literature is that people wind up living with the consequences of their actions. One of the things we accomplish in literature is to examine potential situations, the principles by which one might live in those circumstances, and the consequences of those decisions. Note that I do not limit my study to the Bible, although it is important to me. I also don't limit my study to literary works. The products of natural science are as likely to produce valuable information to me in my decision making process.

I am responsible for what I choose. I reject the excuse that I'm just doing what God commanded.

In this process, I am responsible for what I choose. I reject the excuse that I'm just doing what God commanded. Even if I am doing so, I'm basing the claim on what I believe God commanded. Unless God caught you with a burning bush and told you that I'm right, I have no reason to expect you to believe my claim. When I'm making a decision in the public sphere I should be able to support it with reasoning. I think it's important to be able to defend claims about public policy to people who disagree completely. I know a number of atheists and agnostics who are unafraid to tell me to my face that they find my belief in God somewhere between silly and incomprehensible. At the same time, I can work together with these people because we often agree on public policy goals– separation of church and state, sound science education including evolution, equal protection of the law, environmental issues, public education, and so forth. We may have come to those views from different directions, but we have learned to dialogue about them.

So let's make it simple. I am responsible for my decisions. I look for every form of input I can find, which in my case includes the Bible, I listen to God, I make a decision. Once I make a decision, I take responsibility for the decision.

In this process the Bible functions in two ways: 1) It provides me with extended illustrations of how others interacted with God, and 2) Because I believe that these people interacted with God, I commonly find that if I remove cultural and time factors from the experience, I may find the ideal principle to which God is leading and thus pursue that.

MAKING CHOICES

Choice is extremely important in the Christian life.

[15]But if you don't want to worship the LORD, then choose right now! Will you worship the same idols your ancestors did? Or since you're living on land that once belonged to the Amorites, maybe you'll worship their gods. I won't. My family and I are going to worship and obey the LORD! [16]The people answered:

We could never worship other gods or stop worshiping the LORD. - Joshua 24:15, 16 (CEV)

Choice is extremely important in the Christian life. We choose to accept Jesus as our Savior and Lord, to follow him and become disciples. We choose to resist the evil one, and to ask God's help so we don't have to do it all alone.[29]

---

29 This section is extracted from the pamphlet "Seven Kingdom Principles of Choice," available on the web at http://www.participatorystudyseries.com/pss_full_pamphlet.php?sku=PSS020

The Israelites chose God and promised to obey Him, (Joshua 24:15-16) but they found that promise hard to live up to.

> [1] *"The LORD'S angel went from Gilgal to Bochim and gave the Israelites this message from the LORD: 'I promised your ancestors that I would give this land to their families, and I brought your people here from Egypt. We made an agreement that I promised never to break, [2]and you promised not to make any peace treaties with the other nations that live in the land. Besides that, you agreed to tear down the altars where they sacrifice to their idols. But you didn't keep your promise.*
>
> [3]*And so, I'll stop helping you defeat your enemies. Instead, they will be there to trap you into worshiping their idols.'"* - Judges 2:1-3 (CEV)

God takes small things, like our faith and our choices, and makes big things out of them.

Here are seven principles of choice that can help you choose to follow God and carry out your choice until the end.

1. YOU REAP WHAT YOU SOW.

Jesus taught this in various parables, including the parable of the sower (Matthew 13:1-9). Paul gave the classic statement:

> *You cannot fool God, so don't make a fool of yourself! You will harvest what you plant.* - Galatians 6:7 (CEV)

2. WITH GOD, SMALL MAKES BIG.

God takes small things, like our faith and our choices, and makes big things out of them.

31Jesus told them another story: The kingdom of heaven is like what happens when a farmer plants a mustard seed in a field. 32Although it is the smallest of all seeds, it grows larger than any garden plant and becomes a tree. Birds even come and nest on its branches. — Matthew 13:31, 32 (CEV)

3. YOU ARE NOT THE ONLY SOWER.

Other people are sowing seeds that have an impact on your life, and the enemy of our souls is sowing seeds. But Jesus is faithful to watch and carry out His purposes in the end.

Other people are sowing seeds that have an impact on your life.

24Jesus then told them this story: The kingdom of heaven is like what happened when a farmer scattered good seed in a field. 25But while everyone was sleeping, an enemy came and scattered weed seeds in the field and then left. 26When the plants came up and began to ripen, the farmer's servants could see the weeds. 27The servants came and asked, "Sir, didn't you scatter good seed in your field? Where did these weeds come from?" 28"An enemy did this," he replied. His servants then asked, "Do you want us to go out and pull up the weeds?" 29"No!" he answered. "You might also pull up the wheat. 30Leave the weeds alone until harvest time. Then I'll tell my workers to gather the weeds and tie them up and burn them. But I'll have them store the wheat in my barn."
— Matthew 13:24-30 (CEV)

4. GOD GIVES GIFTS, YOU CHOOSE TO USE THEM.

God promises wisdom to those who ask, and gives it generously (James 1:5). He gave wisdom to Solomon, but while Solomon was able to speak wise sayings and to issue wise judgments to his people, He did not always behave wisely himself. The record of Solomon's life shows that we must choose to use the gifts that God gives us.

> *"A few seeds make a small harvest, but a lot of seeds make a big harvest."* — *2 Corinthians 9:6*

5. CHOOSING SEED TO SOW IS RISKY.

Those who must decide who is a false prophet and who is a true one, have to make a risky choice (Matthew 24:14-30). Elijah had to make a very risky choice on Mt. Carmel (1 Kings 18).

But choosing not to choose is also risky. We must step out and make a choice!

God's promises are often conditioned on obedience to his commands.

6. YOU MUST ENDURE TO THE HARVEST.

The results of your choice may not be apparent as soon as you make it. You may need to wait to see the results.

> *God will bless you, if you don't give up when your faith is being tested. He will reward you with a glorious life, just as he rewards everyone who loves him. - James 1:12 (CEV)*

God's promises are often conditioned on obedience to his commands. This is because God's commands are good, and show us a good way to live.

25You people of Israel accuse me of being unfair! But listen I'm not unfair; you are! 26If good people start doing evil, they must be put to death, because they have sinned. 27And if wicked people start doing right, they will save themselves from punishment. 28They will think about what they've done and stop sinning, and so they won't be put to death. 29But you still say that I am unfair. You are the ones who have done wrong and are unfair! - Ezekiel 18:25-29

7. GRACE OVERCOMES THE LAW OF SOWING AND REAPING.

Jesus illustrated this principle in his reaction to the woman at Simon's feast (Luke 7:36-50). Those who forgive much, love much. God offers his forgiveness to sinners.

"But God proves his love for us in that while we still were sinners Christ died for us." — Romans 5:8 (NRSV)

Grace is offered while we are still sinners. We can break the chain of reaping and sowing where we or our parents have sown evil. God's grace will break the chain and bring forgiveness and love.

"Christ Jesus came into the world to save sinners." - 1 Timothy 1:15 (CEV)

No these commands are nearby and you know them by heart. All you have to do is obey! — Deuteronomy 30:14

RESPONSE TO INERRANCY

Inerrancy is a debate I would prefer to avoid.[30] Unfortunately, most of the discussion about Biblical inspiration today is related in one way to inerrancy. The key question to ask to determine where someone stands on the authority of the Bible is "Do you accept Biblical inerrancy?"

I don't think the issue is nearly as important, and very often I find that if I discuss Biblical interpretation with someone who accepts inerrancy while ignoring that difference, we will often come to similar views on the interpretation of the majority of passages. There will be specific areas in which we will differ, but those will be issues that I consider to be less important.

If I discuss Biblical interpretation with someone who accepts inerrancy while ignoring that difference, we will often come to similar views on the interpretation of the majority of passages.

It is important in discussing inerrancy to determine precisely what is meant by the term. There are many people who claim to believe in this doctrine, and their actual views cover a fairly wide spectrum.

---

30 This chapter has some material that repeats part of previous chapters so that it can be read as an independent statement.

Typically when dealing with academic discussions, the best reference is the Chicago Statement on Biblical Inerrancy.[31]

For those who are less theologically involved, we can use a shorter statement: The Bible, in its autographs, is without error in all that it affirms. Some might prefer "intends to affirm" in order to avoid affirmations that are more in the mind of the reader. Sometimes reflections of the customs of the time are read as affirmative instructions. This inerrancy extends to any type of affirmation, whether scientific, historical, or theological.

It is often frustrating in discussion to deal with the various definitions of inerrancy. Some people, for example, treat every word of the Bible as a specific quotation of God. The middle chapters of Job, for example, contain the speeches of Job's friends which God tells us (Job 38:2) are not correct. Yet many Christians will use quotations from Job's friends as proof texts for doctrinal positions. Their claim is that every word is inspired by God, so they get to use it!

Many Christians will use quotations from Job's friends as proof texts for doctrinal positions. Their claim is that every word is inspired by God, so they get to use it!

The frustration on the other side, I imagine, is the reverse of this. It is likely very annoying to discover that one's opponent is expecting one to support a position one does not accept. In general, this is demonstrated by the assumption that the inerrantist must be a lousy interpreter, unable to deal with different types of literature and sophisticated examination of the purpose of a particular text.

My illustration from Job, for example, applies only to someone who claims that every word of scripture was dictated by God and also claims that it can be used without regard to context. An interpreter can accept inerrancy and agree with my assessment that one should

---

31 You can find a copy of the Chicago Statement at http://www.reformed.org/documents/index.html?mainframe=http://www.ref ormed.org/documents/icbi.html [last accessed 2/14/07].

not make theology out of the speeches of Job's friends, except, of course, as they fit into presenting the overall message of the book. In fact, inerrancy would *require* that interpretation since the inerrant Bible *directly affirms* that those friends did not receive God's approval.

My view of Genesis 1-2 would be a better example. I believe that Genesis 1 is a liturgical description of creation, designed to celebrate God's creative power in a logical fashion. It is not a historical narrative of the events of literal days, nor is it a description of the process of creation, and it was never was intended as such. It is also not primarily chronological.

Many times people respond to this statement by saying that I must not, in that case, believe in Biblical inerrancy. I don't, but my belief about Genesis 1 would not prove it. Someone who accepted my literary classification would not believe that Genesis 1 affirms a six day creation week, any more than a person who hears a pastor affirm "Jesus is Risen" on Easter Sunday morning would believe the pastor is affirming that Jesus rose from the dead within the last few minutes. What the passage affirms depends heavily on what type of literature it is.

Thus inerrancy is neither the doctrine of incompetent Bible students, nor is it a barrier to communication, unless it gets out of place in one's thinking.

Thus inerrancy is neither the doctrine of incompetent Bible students, nor is it a barrier to communication, unless it gets out of place in one's thinking. There are some folks who believe all involved in discussing the Bible must first believe in Biblical inerrancy. They elevate the form of communication over the substance, and I would argue that they elevate what is created above the creator and are guilty of bibliolatry.[32]

---

32 Be very careful in accusing others of bibliolatry. It is not bibliolatry to have a very high view of inspiration, to respect God's written word very highly, and to defend it from attacks. Bibliolatry should be reserved for making the

Inerrancy and Communication

Before we go on to discuss the doctrine of inerrancy in further detail, let's consider again the one-ended telephone cord. Inerrancy in its most common form simply states that the autographs, the texts as written by the original writers before they were copied, are without error. We don't have any of those autographs. All we have are copies of copies. To the believer in inerrancy, it is acceptable for the copies to contain errors, just so long as we uphold our doctrine of God by maintaining that at some point there was no error.

The doctrine of inerrancy tends to the treat the cord as having only one end. Because inerrancy is attributed to the autographs, but we have no autographs, errors are OK in the text of the Bible, just so long as they were not introduced by the original writers. Anyone can make a mistake except for them. Why are errors more important if they are introduced when God speaks to a prophet, than they are if they are introduced by a copyist? I believe the reason is simply that inerrancy is designed more to protect the doctrine of God than it is to protect the integrity of God's communication with humanity. God's communication must be perfect.

> *God cannot communicate perfectly if the message is not received perfectly.*

But communication involves two persons. The cord has two ends. God cannot communicate perfectly if the message is not received perfectly. And if the message is only received perfectly by the original prophet (conveniently unavailable to check), but not by later readers, than how is that perfect communication? That, in my view, is the weakness in this doctrine. It does not deal with how we can know God's will specifically, but rather deals only with God's side of the equation. The only people assumed to know God's will are the original recipients.

Bible some kind of magic talisman, or for putting the book ahead of God, who is its source.

So the first answer to my question is simply, no. The doctrine of inerrancy is not relevant, because it relates to something I do not have. How can it be important to me that something that I do not have and cannot read does not contain errors?

WHAT GOOD IS YOUR BIBLE?

The single most common response I get to my view of inerrancy is this: "Then why study and teach the Bible?"

This question illustrates a portion of the problem. The value of the Bible has become attached in people's thinking to the notion of inerrancy. Imagine for a moment that, instead of announcing that I'm a Bible teacher, I were to say, "I teach English literature."

Someone asks, "Do you consider Shakespeare inerrant?"

"No, I don't," I respond, looking puzzled.

"Then why do you teach English literature?"

Bible is the only subject in which a Christian teacher is expected to make the claim that the subject matter source is without error of any kind

The question sounds ridiculous in that context. (We could use any English author in the question.) Now many Christians may be thinking about now, "But the Bible is more important than Shakespeare, or any of those other English authors." I'm not disagreeing with that assessment. I believe that the Bible is extremely important. At a minimum it is important because of the strong influence it has had on culture and literature. But the point remains, that Bible is the only subject in which a Christian teacher is expected to make the claim that the subject matter source is without error of any kind, whether or not that error is related to the subject matter at issue.

Does this mean that I believe the Bible is limited to its value as literature? No, not at all. What I mean is that the Bible is a valuable piece of literature even if not regarded as inerrant. The value of the

Bible does not lie in being without error, but in conveying God's message. In addition, the Bible contains great literature, which should be of valuable even if one didn't regard it as divinely inspired.

In practice, I find that I interpret most passages in the same way as other interpreters who do believe in inerrancy (provided it is the inerrancy specified in the Chicago Statement on Biblical Inerrancy). I have actually been asked just what is the difference in my view by some who have compared notes on many controversial passages. I see my understanding of Biblical inerrancy not as a solution to "problems"-most of which I find very enlightening when studied-but rather an attitude. My attitude toward scripture is to listen to God speaking to a human audience. Grace regards the needs of the human audience more than a need to assert the divine attribute of infallibility. In other words, God speaks in a way in which we can hear right now even if some later generation might regard that message as flawed because of some new discovery. And you can be certain that if the Lord doesn't return first, our current understanding of science will move so much that the way we see scripture today will seem naïve and unscientific. God was gracious to speak in a way that the ancients could understand, and he's gracious to help us understand that message now through the power of the Spirit.

I believe that the Bible is the result of God interacting with people, and that it has been providentially protected by God.

I believe that the Bible is the result of God interacting with people, and that it has been providentially protected by God. This means that errors and contradictions are there because God permitted. God could have exercised more intense control over the process, but he did not.

I would note two types of error especially. First, there are those cases of inadvertent written error. An example would be the ages of certain kings in the records of Kings and Chronicles. These may be copyists' errors (one proposed solution) but I don't believe they are of concern whether they occurred in the royal records of Judah and Israel, were the fault of the compiler of Kings or Chronicles, or were committed by an early copyist. They simply have no impact on the meaning of the book. Second, there are intentional statements that we regard as errors in the modern world. An example would be the listing of bats as birds in Leviticus 11:19. (The categories used here are simply different than ours.)

I believe that God speaks to people in the cultural and historical setting in which he finds them. Jesus didn't use divine knowledge in order to spice up his parables with aircraft, for example. But I go further. I believe he speaks using the cosmology and historical knowledge of the time wherever that improves communication to the original audience. In this case we may regard something as a historical or scientific error, but correction of that error would harm communication to the original audience.

I believe that God speaks to people in the cultural and historical setting in which he finds them.

The inspiration of the Bible differs from that of other books. I believe that God has worked in inspiring the writers, in the collection and copying of the work, and continues to work in the process of translation. As a result I believe the Bible conveys God's message in the way that he wants it conveyed.

However, this argument functions in the context of Christian theology. It is commonly held that the process of bringing someone into faith in Jesus Christ is a matter of first convincing him that the Bible is true, and then using the Bible to convince him of the specific doctrines of the Christian faith. I would suggest instead that experience is first in the sharing of the good news. We first share the testimony of our experience, and when and if the sharing of our experience brings a desire for similar experience, then we share the theological expression of that experience.

Our present method in the west is based on the strong cultural position of the Bible in which many people who are not active in church life or who don't call themselves Christians still hold some sort of reverence for the Bible. This allows us to start with the Bible. The lack of success of modern Christianity with populations that lack this Biblical background I believe results from replacing a living experience of God with a set of doctrinal postulates, most of which only make sense in the context of a personal experience with God. In other words, I see this doctrinal approach as having a form of godliness, but denying its power (2 Timothy 3:5).

We can, for example, teach theology, church history, counseling, church administration, worship, and many similar topics without necessarily referring to an inerrant source. We also include many very errant sources in our Bible study and find value in them. Nobody has any problem with this. But our view of the Bible has become binary: Either it is inerrant or it is useless and of no authority.

I do not believe that using an inappropriate standard to judge any piece of literature is a mark of respect for that literature.

Others object that while there may be problems with the doctrine of inerrancy, it seems inappropriate to argue against excessive reverence. Reverence is good, and if people go a bit overboard, what problem is there? "Perhaps inerrantists are overstating their case, but they certainly do have respect for the text," these folks say.

I do not believe that using an inappropriate standard to judge any piece of literature is a mark of respect for that literature. I'm certain inerrantists do indeed have great respect for the scriptures, but the question is whether or not the standard they are applying to the scriptures is an appropriate one. Note again that I'm not talking about the standard being too high; rather I'm talking about it simply being the wrong one. Is their respect for the scriptures as they are, or as they imagine them to be?

Indeed I'm quite certain most of those who accept inerrancy would not be sympathetic to a suggestion that we tolerate their view just because it isn't harmful. They believe that inerrancy is the truth, and would want it accepted or rejected on that basis.

Let me illustrate with a piece of literature for which I have great respect, but which nobody of my acquaintance considers inerrant, J. R. R. Tolkien's "Lord of the Rings." Suppose someone takes this series and determines that it indeed describes a real realm or universe, and that the description is inerrant. He begins to describe how the earth in its present state developed from the world of Middle Earth and insists that every principle, moral or otherwise, contained in the trilogy is binding and totally without error. He then insists that everyone who says that the books are "merely" great literature, fine and uplifting reading, is showing disrespect for them, because they are truly inerrant, the words of a prophet. Who is showing respect for Tolkien's work? Clearly the person who respects and appreciates it for what it is.

The Bible is actually a collection of many types of literature, including fiction.

Some people respond immediately by asking whether I believe the Bible is fiction. If that is your response, look again at the illustration before you continue. I am not claiming that the Bible is fiction. It is actually a collection of many types of literature, including fiction. My purpose in the illustration is not to show what the Bible actually is, but to show that one respects a literary work by appreciating what it actually is, not by claiming it is something else, however uplifting that something else might claim to be. Thus, if the Bible is not inerrant, or if in some other way it is inappropriate to judge it by the standard of inerrancy, then we do not show respect for it by making that claim.

Let me make one further point. If the Bible is not inerrant, we put people's faith in jeopardy by teaching that it is.

Let me illustrate what I mean. Supposing that I tell someone that the inspiration of the Bible is such that no matter what their need for guidance, they can pray, and then let their Bible fall open in front of them, place their finger on a verse, and they will get guidance for the immediate future from that verse.

Despite the fact that many pastors and teachers warn against such a teaching, there are many people who have tried it, and there are many stories floating around Christian circles that tell how someone was guided using this method.

What will happen when that person uses this method and finds a text that he cannot relate to his situation at all. What will happen when he finds a verse that gives him incorrect guidance?

We run the risk that the believer who was trusting in the method will discard the Bible because it has proven untrustworthy. You see, the fact is that this method is not one that God ordained for regular use, though I do believe he has honored some requests presented in this manner. But as soon as this guidance fails, we run the risk that the believer who was trusting in the method will discard the Bible because it has proven untrustworthy. We would hope that they would find a more mature understanding of the purpose of the Bible, but we cannot be sure of that.

Now inerrancy is a more subtle and nuanced issue, but I believe the same argument would apply to teaching it unless you truly believe it is true and that it will stand up to scrutiny. Thus I reject any idea of teaching something I do not believe is true simply because it is a type of belief that is pious or reverent.

The question then is, what is the Bible? Once we have determined that, we can ask: What is its role and authority? How should we approach it?

TERMINOLOGY AND APPROACH

I will first indicate why some traditional models to fail to adequately handle the objective evidence and the experience of Christian individuals with God and the Bible. First let me list and define some approaches as I understand them.

Verbal Dictation - the idea that God, through the Holy Spirit, dictated the very words of scripture, such that it is proper to say that these are the actual words of God. People who hold this idea will normally reject any notion that the personality, attitudes and culture of the prophet has any impact on the meaning of the text nor does the nature of the audience. Often the words of scripture as they occur are applied to situations far different than those in which they were spoken.

Verbal Plenary Inspiration - while rejecting the notion of verbal dictation people who hold this doctrine believe that every word is protected by God. Neither the prophet's views, nor those of the audience have real impact. (See below under Communications Model, page .)

Hard Inerrancy - no statement in the Bible can contain false information of any type.

Soft Inerrancy - the Bible is always inerrant in that which it intends to state. Thus, while that which is being communicated must be accurate, the idea could be communicated using ideas which are current in the surrounding culture. This is the version of inerrancy which I understand most American evangelicals to espouse.

> *While that which is being communicated must be accurate, the idea could be communicated using ideas which are current in the surrounding culture.*

Note that there is a difference between a small group of people who hold to inerrancy of a particular translation, usually the King James Version, and those who hold to inerrancy of the autographs. Those who hold a doctrine of inerrancy of the autographs will generally admit that there have been errors in copying and transmission but consider these errors negligible and as having no impact on teachings necessary to salvation. There is an intermediate position which would maintain the inerrancy of the majority text [Maj] (or sometimes of the Textus Receptus[TR]) for the New Testament, and of the Masoretic Text [MT] for the Tanak.

The difference between the approach to the inerrancy of the autographs or of a modern text or version may be illustrated by the handling of differences between the age of Jehoiachin at his accession to the throne of Judah. In the KJV (and in the MT on which it is based) 2 Chronicles 36:9 lists Jehoiachin's age as eight years, while 2 Kings 24:8 lists his age as 18. (A soft inerrantist might not find this issue worth dealing with, but some do.) If one checks the modern versions one will find in many cases, either in the text of 2 Chronicles 36:9 or in a note at that passage that some versions read "18" there as well. The New Century Version [NCV] reads "18" without any note.

It is quite easy to claim that the problem is a copyist's error. These passages do not pose any difficulty for one who believes in the inerrancy of the autographs, however, because it is quite easy to claim that the problem is a copyist's error. One who believes in inerrancy of the KJV, or of the MT on which it is based, must explain the difference in ages in some way. These descriptions can become extremely fanciful.

WHY NOT INERRANCY?

It is not my purpose to suggest that the Bible is unsuitable for its purpose or lacking in authority, thus you will find here only a limited list of errors or contradictions, along with how my approach to inspiration can be used to deal with them. My purpose is to show why I feel that inerrancy is inadequate to the task and what approach I espouse as an alternative.

What is this task?

> *"All inspired scripture has its use for teaching the truth and refuting error, or for reformation of manners and discipline in right living, so that the man of God may*

be capable and equipped for good work of every kind."
(2 Timothy 3:16 (REB)

The New International Version uses the alternate translation: "All scripture is God-breathed and is useful for teaching, rebuking, correcting and training in righteousness, so that the man of God may be thoroughly equipped for every good work." Either translation is workable for what I am about to suggest. This is probably the most quoted Biblical statement on the scriptures. In my view this text in fact defines what a complete view of inspiration must entail.

First, it discusses "all scripture" or "all inspired scripture." Most Christians accept the books of the canon as inspired. Only a view of inspiration which shows how all scripture is useful will coincide with this statement. (Note here that I am aware that 2 Timothy was written before the canon as we know it was accepted. To apply the text, one must both accept the validity of the verse itself, and also the validity of the process of canonization. In its original context, however, this text did not refer to the canon of scripture as accepted by either Protestants or Roman Catholics.)

I believe that most Christians discard the books of Leviticus, Numbers and large portions of Exodus and Deuteronomy.

In practice, however, many Christians do not really accept everything in the scriptures as profitable. For example, I believe that most Christians discard the books of Leviticus, Numbers and large portions of Exodus and Deuteronomy. I'm sure some will protest that they do not such thing, but that they view these things as pointing to Christ and done away with at the cross. But how much profit do you get from them in that case? Do we even seriously read and study them? If, in the words of Paul, the law was a schoolmaster, it was a master whose lectures we no longer remember.

Second, it requires a view of the text which sees all of scripture as profitable for these various goals. But in what way are certain passages profitable? If we go to the scripture to get doctrine, of what value are the following?

> *Everything that confronts them, everything is futile, since one and the same fate comes to all, just and unjust alike, good and bad, ritually clean and unclean, to the one who offers sacrifice and to the one who does not. The good and the sinner fare alike, he who can take an oath and he who dares not* — Ecclesiastes *9:1b-2 (REB)*

> *"Babylon, Babylon the destroyer, happy is he who repays you for what you did to us! Happy is he who seizes your babes and dashes them against a rock"* — Psalm *137:8,9 (REB)*

In what way are these texts profitable? Or in Numbers 31, after the people have returned from attacking Midian, and bring with them alive the women and children from the conquered territories: "Now kill every male child, and kill every woman who has had intercourse with a man, but you may spare for yourselves every woman among them who has not had intercourse." (Numbers 31:17)

In what way are these texts profitable? Under a view of the scriptures which finds in them largely a compendium of doctrine, I see very little use.

Lastly, I think a valid view of inspiration must take into account the purpose of the entire collection. Why, in fact, do we want inspired writings at all. The answer given in 2 Timothy 3:17 is: ". . . so that the man of God may be capable and equipped for good work of every kind." Here is a final goal. I note that verse 17 is very often ignored by those who quote this passage. They are especially interested in how the Bible functions as a vehicle for bringing them doctrine, and for validating that doctrine. It is with the doctrinal authority of the scriptures that they are most concerned. But the expressed concern of this text is with the practical goal.

Now some people reading this section may be thinking that I am using circular reasoning here by looking within the Bible for the characteristics I wish to see comprehended by a view of inspiration. Indeed I am being circular. But I agree with the position stated in this scripture. Let me state these principles concerning inspired writings out in non-scriptural terms. In looking at a set of works which we see as authoritative, we need to ask in what way the entire collection is authoritative. Why, in fact, the entire collection? Because if we answer the question by making part of the collection not scripture, then we are simply redefining the question. In addition, not all sections of scripture need be authoritative in the same way. (See below for a further discussion of the term "authoritative".) Secondly, if something is authoritative, we need to see its function, or in what way it is authoritative. A set of regulations is defined in terms of accomplishing a particular task or managing a particular process. Each has its context and basis. As Christians, we generally claim the Bible as an authority. Authority for what? Thirdly, I believe we need to look at a final goal for our community. If the Bible is an authority in our community, what is it that we intend to accomplish by means of following or observing that authority.

What characteristics should a divine revelation have?

There is a problem in general with circular reasoning in dealing with a written or verbal revelation in all cases, because there is no separate standard by which one can judge a revelation. What characteristics should a divine revelation have? We don't know unless we find out from within a divine revelation. How should we determine the truth of any particular item of divine revelation? Again, we look to divine revelation. In 1 Kings 22, Ahab and Jehoshaphat are presented with this problem. With many people claiming to speak for God, yet saying different things, the audience was confronted with the need to choose which message to regard as divine. Both Jeremiah (Jeremiah 23) and Ezekiel (Ezekiel 14) were confronted with a similar situation. How were the people to choose the correct message? One couldn't do so by checking the fulfillment of the prophecies, as that would be too late to make the correct choice.

I discern two major problems with the doctrine of inerrancy, derived from these observations.

First, the doctrine of inerrancy leads to a view of the text as a series of statements, suitable for fashioning into doctrines, which can then be treated as true or false. This view appears to me to contradict the very nature of the text, most of which is dedicated to issues which do not fashion readily into doctrines. I suspect this view of greatly reducing the real study of the scriptures, because such a small portion of the scriptures appear useful in this model. One seems more knowledgeable of the scriptures when one can quote the proof texts for one's doctrines, but this knowledge is of a small portion of the whole.

The only way the Bible could be objectively proven to be the word of God would be if we had something other than the Bible which was an already accepted standard to which we could compare it.

Second, I believe this view fails on the basis of standard. By what standard does one test an inerrant scripture? I have been presented with the view that if one does not believe that all of scripture is inerrant, that one is left without an objective basis for proving scripture. The conviction of the inerrancy of scripture, however, must come from errant sources, such as scientific and archaeological study. The only way the Bible could be objectively proven to be the word of God would be if we had something other than the Bible which was an already accepted standard to which we could compare it.

The fact is, unfortunately, that the "errant" sources to which we compare inerrant scripture do not tend to support its inerrancy. If one takes the dominant trends in the various fields of history, archeology, geology, and others, one will find that these trends tend to differ from the content of the Bible. One can object that we need "true" science and the "right" results, which will support the Bible. And as long as one chooses these sources according to whether or not they support the Bible, one will, of course, find support. But choosing only that evidence which supports one's thesis is not an objective approach.

My objections here do not prove that the Bible is not inerrant. What they do show, I believe, is that we have no way of determining whether the Bible is inerrant because we lack any accepted, inerrant standard to which to compare it. In addition, the best judgment of the human sources we have available is that the Bible is not without error.

The bloody passages do not project an ideal.

I believe that it is very unlikely that anyone who starts a study of the Bible without a pre-existing bias in favor of inerrancy will determine that it is inerrant. There are a number of fine people who would probably disagree with me on this point, among whom I include Dr. Gleason Archer, and Dr. Norman Geisler. I am led to believe that individuals who approach the study of the Bible from a skeptical view, and are then converted to Christianity by their study, and often become advocates of inerrancy, in fact encounter God, the real authority, in their study, and their discovery of inerrancy follows from that. I am not challenging their experience, sincerity or honesty on that basis, but I would ask a similar favor for those of us who cannot honestly accept the inerrancy of scripture and nonetheless have encountered God.

SOME PRACTICAL EXAMPLES

How do I apply this idea to dealing with Biblical problem passages. I will deal with some briefly by category as carrying out extended exegesis on each passage is beyond the scope of this paper.

The Bloody Passages

These include Numbers 31 (command to kill all but the virgin girls), Psalm 137:8,9 (rejoicing over the death of an enemy's children), and Judges 5 (celebrating treachery and murder of a guest). One could place beside these the rather bloody stories of Judges 17-21. In these cases I read, as always the experience and state of the people at the time. These are not projections of an ideal. As a matter of fact the Bible rarely projects an ideal and because of this it can be a very dangerous book in the hands of a thoughtless person. As part of the total record of the community of faith, this is simply authentic. I know of no other tradition which is as self-critical as is that of the Hebrew scriptures.

This is a problem for those with a view of verbal dictation, but for nobody else. Let me illustrate this approach further using 1 Samuel 24 and 1 Chronicles 21. In the first of these passages David's choice to number Israel is credited to God's moving and in the second to Satan. (I'm indebted to Alden Thompson in his book "Inspiration" for this illustration.)[33] I am not so much interested in explaining who really did it, as in noticing that the attribution of the action is different in the one written earlier. This attribution reflects a distinctly human understanding of the cause of the event in each case.

Technical Errors

For example, Matthew 27:9, a quote which is either composite or taken from Zechariah is attributed to Jeremiah. I can hardly awaken an interest in this one, but let me just note that in Hebrews 2:6, the author appears to be unable to remember the source of a quotation at all. This is a problem for those with a view of verbal dictation, but for nobody else.

---

33 Thompson, Alden. Inspiration: Hard Questions, Honest Answers. Hagerstown, MD: Review and Herald Publishing Association, 1991, pp. 173-175.

An additional apparent technical error comes from Hebrews:

> *3 Behind the second curtain was a tent called the Holy of Holies. 4 In it stood the golden altar of incense and the ark of the covenant overlaid on all sides with gold, in which there were a golden urn holding the manna, and Aaron's rod that budded, and the tablets of the covenant; 5 above it were the cherubim of glory overshadowing the mercy seat. Of these things we cannot speak now in detail. — Hebrews 9:3-5 (NRSV)*

So what's wrong with this? The golden altar, also known as the altar of incense was actually in the outer compartment, and not the inner compartment with the ark of the covenant.

Now this error, or perhaps simple looseness in the way the tabernacle is described has no impact on the message of the passage, but if one is to take this passage as a detailed technical description, it is not an accurate one.

This error has no impact on the message of the passage.

Quotations

These fall into two categories, first quotations of and allusions to literature which is considered uninspired, and second quotations which appear to be taken out of context or with a meaning which would not have been attached to them by the original author.

In the first category we have Jude 14, which is quoted from the book of Enoch. I know of nobody who would consider the book of Enoch authoritative or authentic, though under the view of experience presented here it does constitute a part of the tradition and experience of those who became Christians, yet Jude quotes it as authoritative and attributes it to the patriarch Enoch. "It was against them that Enoch, the seventh in descent from Adam, prophesied when he said: " I saw the Lord come with his myriads of angels, . . ."

This quotation comes from Enoch 60:8. I would give more than one possible solution to this. First, that Jude may have regarded the book of Enoch as authoritative. In looking at the book of Jude, we look for his message, and how he brought it. Second, it may be that, whatever Jude thought about the book of Enoch, his audience considered it authoritative. In any case I don't believe that quoting from a book authenticates the content of the book from which the material is quoted.

In the second category we have usages such as that of Hosea 11:1 by Matthew 2:15 which was discussed earlier. This is simply a part of Matthew's approach to scripture and it has some relation to the entire approach to interpretation of his time.

In modern times we tend to want a clear divide between the values conveyed by myth and literal, narrative history.

In dismissing the importance of these types of problems from the point of view of inspiration I am in no way dismissing them as being of no interest. They are the kinds of problems which led me to the view which I have of inspiration. If I felt that the use of quotations by Biblical writers was scientific and always in context, I would not look for a reason why it was not! It is because of these types of problems, however, that I reject the notion of a purely divine revelation, that is, of words given by or dictated by God.

INERRANCY AND FAITH

Is the way we understand literal meaning versus the mythical meaning today different from what it used to be? For example, would ancient readers have been less likely to see a substantial division between a literal reading of Genesis 1 (a seven day creation week) and a spiritual one?

This is a topic that is much on my mind lately as I worked on manuscript for this book. I think there is a difference between the way we see this and the way the ancients did. The reason that conclusion is controversial is that we have strong statements about the truth and accuracy of scripture that predate inerrancy. So what is happening here?

Well, we have not merely a shift in the "popular epistemology" (I prefer this to worldview) of Christianity, but of the map on which epistemologies are arranged. The categories of "myth" and "truth" were not so divided as they are in popular perception. Minor differences in the gospels didn't bother people a few centuries ago like they bother people now because that was not where their focus was. The very claim to truth doesn't mean the same to an inerrantist that it did then. The interesting thing is that a hard-line inerrantist (and there are many "soft" versions) shares with most atheists one point: Both require that all their beliefs be fully supported by objective evidence; no personal experiences need apply.

I think that in that fight atheism wins for several reasons. One is that if you make the supernatural completely subject to scientific examination, it is no longer supernatural; it's just a somewhat more complex natural. In other words, if we allow the discussion to be limited to scientific study, we will never find the supernatural. The word "supernatural" is a bit iffy here because I refer to anything spiritual, and "supernatural" carries a lot of freight I'd like to leave behind, but I'm not certain of a better word.

You can't really get "spiritual benefit" into the lab, much less under the microscope.

Another reason is that phenomena that are more probable and easier to get to are more likely to amass objective evidence. Further, both views require that the observer potentially can get all the facts in hand, and atheists are more consistent about that.

Thus without a leap of faith or something similar, I think religious faith or spirituality is dead in the long run. My more evidence conscious friends may regard me as out on a limb that I've already sawn off, but I think they're sitting on a limb they imagine for themselves. Who's going to fall first?

This applies to inerrancy because the one critical point inerrancy gives to its advocates is the ability to test the Bible. You can't really get "spiritual benefit" into the lab, much less under the microscope. Historical and logical errors are a different matter. So inerrantists make logical consistency along with scientific and historical accuracy the test of scriptures. But such things are totally within a human framework. Humans can write texts that are logically consistent and historically and scientifically accurate. In fact, they can write texts that require substantially less explanation than inerrantists are required to provide for the Bible. Just read any handbook on dealing with Biblical errors, and you'll see the flexibility that is permitted in order to "prove" the Bible.

Now what inerrantists tell me is that by conceding factual, logical, and even theological error in the Bible, I've given away the whole shop. But I think we still start at the same point. After they have worked for years explaining every possible contradiction and error, they still don't have any basis to say the book is divine. If I could have the time and flexibility they take with explanations, I could make the "Lord of the Rings" into scripture and incidentally have lots of fun on the way!

After they have worked for years explaining every possible contradiction and error, they still don't have any basis to say the book is divine.

So what makes a piece of writing "divine" or "inspired" if a lack of logical or factual errors doesn't get us there? Well, that's where I think there absolutely must be a leap of faith. You have to start somewhere, because if God is something more than his universe, and we are in and of this universe, then we can't have something that is also merely in this universe that is a clear standard for what is divine, because no matter what that might be, the divine would have to transcend it.

That leaves me with two points. First, I look for the existence of God experientially, and that's where faith comes in. For me, my choice to return to Christianity after testing other waters was not so much a conversion **to** belief as a realization that I already **did** believe. Second, my acceptance of the Bible as sacred literature comes afterward, because I detect the voice of God in it based on that existing faith experience.

This is also why I rarely have extensive debates about belief with atheists or agnostics. I understand and empathize with their point of view. Sometimes I'm even logically drawn toward it. But sort of like Harrison Ford's Indiana Jones going through the tests in quest of the grail, I already took the step and the bridge appeared under my foot, so here I am. I may even shake my head at the stuff that people who claimed to know God did back in ancient times, but I think they were struggling toward the same divine presence that I am.

A willingness to admit one does not know is an important part of any study of theology.

I just picked up the copy of "The God Delusion" from the library, which I had to put on hold in order to snag. I'm afraid I know much of what Dawkins says already, from my prior reading of his works, but it doesn't have any impact. He thinks people like me are pretty dense for believing something without evidence, and I have to plead guilty. There is a step—a very long step—between where I am now and the last evidence. It's not that there is no evidence, but just not enough, nor do I believe there can be. If there is actually enough evidence for it, it's not God.

CONCLUSION

The primary goal of authority in spiritual matters is in developing the personal experience with God. A believer recognizes the authority in something written or spoken because the message matches what is given by the spirit to the individual. We say with Paul that "It is by declaring the truth openly that we recommend ourselves to the conscience of our fellow-men in the sight of God." (2 Corinthians 4:2b). We maintain an objectivity and a continuity by comparing our experience not just with the present, but with the experience of the community as a whole. We do not, however, have an external, objective standard by which we can force these conclusions upon anyone else. A willingness to admit one does not know is an important part of any study of theology.

As for the Bible I believe we have this treasure in earthenware jars (2 Corinthians 4:7). It is the guidance of God in the experience of the community of faith as a whole which is recorded, and which has been selected through the understanding and use. Inspiration is not just of a writer, but it also requires an audience to hear and to recognize what has been said.

It is the combination of the experience, the writing, and the understanding of the audience which constitutes the word of God in the community of faith.

RESPONSE TO <u>TOGETHER FOR THE GOSPEL</u> ON SCRIPTURE

The Together for the Gospel (T4G) statement[34] was written and signed by four pastors and scholars, J. Ligon Duncan III, Mark E. Dever, C. J. Mahaney, and R. Albert Mohler, Jr. This statement is so substantially shaping the debate about scripture amongst conservative Christians, that I would like to respond to it specifically. It's view of scripture differs in almost all ways from mine, but I think that while discussing canon these difference will be the clearest.

> *This statement is substantially shaping the debate about scripture amongst conservative Christians.*

ARTICLE I

This article reads:

> We affirm that the sole authority for the Church is the Bible, verbally inspired, inerrant, infallible, and totally sufficient and trustworthy.

---

34 Together for the Gospel, from URL http://www.t4g.org/T4TG-statement.pdf, last accessed 3/8/07.

> We deny that the Bible is a mere witness to the divine revelation, or that any portion of Scripture is marked by error or the effects of human sinfulness.

I find myself so fundamentally in disagreement with this article that practically every word requires some sort of response. The basics of that response will occur elsewhere in this book.

> We affirm that the sole authority for the Church is the Bible,

It's interesting that the major portion of the history of faith in the world in general occurred without the Bible, and even more without the Bible as we have it today. If the Bible is the sole authority, God took his time about creating that sole authority. Where in the Bible is there a statement that the Bible is the sole authority? If one is to hold to this exclusive variety of *sola scriptura* then there should be a basis in scripture for:

Where in the Bible is there a statement that the Bible is the sole authority?

- The canon of scripture, which is nowhere specified in scripture
- The use and interpretation of scripture, again unspecified, though we have examples of some interesting approaches
- The precise text of scripture.

I don't think that these issues make it impossible to view the Bible as authoritative. The Bible is the foundation of my faith, but then I don't make any claim that the Bible is the *exclusive* authority. One of the key errors that stands behind the T4G view is the understanding that when the Bible refers to the "word of God" one can apply all those things that are attributed to "the word" to the Bible.

Throughout Biblical history the church was led by prophets, apostles, and other leaders who were said to be in some sort of communion with God. There is no indication of a time when a collection of literature was or would become the sole authority. This does not mean that the Bible is not fundamental, or that it is not extremely important, or that it does not convey God's word. In fact, I would say that its authority is foundational, but it provides the foundation for a structure. The Christian church is not founded on a book, but on a person.

> verbally inspired, inerrant, infallible, and totally sufficient and trustworthy.

You will search the Bible in vain for scriptures that actually affirm these doctrines. Skipping over the more complex theological definitions, *verbally inspired* is generally understood to mean that the words of scripture, and not just the thoughts or the message, is inspired. Some of those who hold that the Bible is verbally inspired also hold that it was verbally dictated, that God provided the very words of scripture to the prophet. Others hold that God protects the words so that we can safely say they are God's words, even though the personality of writers show through. The end result is very similar, because one assumes that each word is there by God's direct choice; not God's choice of a writer or a message, but his choice of a specific word.

Literal translation sacrifices meaning in favor of form.

This obviously presents a problem for translators because the very words of God occur only in the source languages in that case. Every translation takes from the people the very words of God and replaces them with the words of a translator or translation committee. Those who hold a verbal view of inspiration often advocate literal Bible translation, because it remains closest to the words of the original. But this view sacrifices the *meaning* in favor of the *form*.

Inerrancy is normally understood as the claim that the Biblical autographs are without error in all it affirms, no matter what the topic, thus including science and history. A minority will hold that a particular translation or manuscript contains the perfect word of God. This latter position is clearly nonsense, because no matter what translation or manuscript one chooses, one also excludes the majority of the readers of the Bible throughout history from having such an inerrant scripture. *Inerrancy of the autographs* suffers from a lack of any autographs by which one might check the claim. If God was concerned that the autographs be without error, he was apparently inexplicably unconcerned with seeing that the actual copies that you and I can read are without error.

Infallibility is a vacuous claim to make about a book, simply because the book does not, in fact, do anything. Interpretations can clearly be in error. It seems more important to me to understand how people get information from the book. Infallibility that is inaccessible is of little interest, and one need only read a few commentaries or books on Biblical theology to see that infallibility is apparently inaccessible.

The Bible is sufficient for its purpose. We have to make sure we understand what that purpose is.

Totally sufficient and trustworthy causes me to wonder what it is that the Bible is totally sufficient for. Normally theologians will say "totally sufficient for salvation," though many will maintain that under appropriate circumstances considerably less than that is sufficient. This claim seems to me to hardly go beyond saying that the Bible is what it is. I agree! And I think it is sufficient to its purpose. I also find it trustworthy, provided we are careful to understand what its purpose is. It is not trustworthy, for example, as a science text. That's not a criticism, just an observation. It was never intended as a science text. It does not replace one's personal communion with God. Again, it was never intended to.

More important than the items of definition I have pointed out is a common failing of all these claims about scripture: They all rely on a particular approach to developing a Biblical theology of the Bible. The common approach is to take a passage such as 1 Peter 2:19-21 or

2 Timothy 3:16, and then decide on the basis of these texts what the Bible **ought to be**. Other than the circularity of this approach, which can be ameliorated through other theological approaches, I find it interesting that in the face of a substantial history of the Bible and how it came to be, so many theologians prefer to define what they **want** it to be, rather than simply observing what it is.

2 Timothy 3:16 provides us with the word "theopneustos" or "God-breathed" which has been made to carry a great deal of freight. But when God breathed into Adam he didn't make him inerrant, he made him alive. What exactly is the content of a text that is God-breathed? But this issue applies much more to verbal inspiration. The evidence against verbal inspiration is very strong in the text and the history itself. There are certainly words that are attributed to God, but there are also words that are clearly **not** attributed to God. The synoptic problem presents us with clear evidence that the gospel writers copied from one another, that there are different sources in the Pentateuch, Samuel, and Kings, just as examples.

I know that one can live by faith because Abraham, Moses, and Jesus did.

Now for the denials:

> We deny that the Bible is a mere witness to the divine revelation,

I don't get the phrase "mere witness." To me, the most wonderful thing about the Bible is that it is a witness to divine revelation and to divine action in history. The fact that it is written by humans who are subject to error as I am makes it much more accessible. I know that one can live by faith because Abraham, Moses, and Jesus did. This witness is not *mere,* it is critical. The author of Hebrews uses it as a showcase for his argument in Hebrews 11.

> or that any portion of Scripture is marked by error or the effects of human sinfulness.

But the copies that we actually have are marked by error. I do not mean extensive error, but Biblical inerrantists will not allow the smallest error in the autographs, and yet are satisfied with a 98% or 99% accurate copy. Of course one can't determine that for certain again, because we don't have the autographs. I don't think this is a serious problem for Bible study, interpretation, and application, but that is because I don't believe that inerrancy is relevant to those issues at all.

The effects of human sinfulness are all around us. The very fact that we need to hear the word through prophets or read it in books is the result of sin and our separation from God. Without human sinfulness there would be no need for the Bible at all.

The effects of human sinfulness are all around us.
Inspiration is an incarnational process, God breathing life into imperfect words in imperfect human language to be preserved imperfectly by imperfect copyists, read imperfectly by imperfect readers, preached by imperfect preachers, and discussed by very imperfect writers such as myself.

ARTICLE II

We affirm that the authority and sufficiency of Scripture extends to the entire Bible, and therefore that the Bible is our final authority for all doctrine and practice.

We deny that any portion of the Bible is to be used in an effort to deny the truthfulness or trustworthiness of any other portion. We further deny any effort to identify a canon within the canon or, for example, to set the words of Jesus against the writings of Paul.

I agree that the authority and sufficiency (whatever that means) of scripture extends to all of scripture, but for reasons I have previously stated, I do not agree that the Bible is our sole source of doctrine. The key to this article, however, comes in the denials, which show that it is intended to respond to the idea of a "personal canon" or a "canon within a canon." Now I think the notion of a "personal canon" is logically questionable. A "canon" is a set of writings held by a community to be authoritative in some formal sense, such as church law. Thus a "personal canon" can be held to be an oxymoron. But there is a very practical idea that is also often intended by the term; individuals build their spiritual life with different emphases on different portions of the scripture.

One could argue that the individual has a "canon" which is authoritative for him, and which includes all the written works that he regards a authoritative. But in that case, why have a canon at all? The individual is clearly the one exercising the authority to choose what is authoritative and what is not. What will he do if one of those books says something with which he disagrees?

God chose to give the scriptures through different writers at different times and in different places.

As an example, other than the gospels, which I regard as central, I spend more time on the average reading the Pentateuch from the Old Testament and the general epistles, especially Hebrews from the New Testament. My wife tends to read more of the Psalms, some prophets, and her New testament reading other than the gospels generally comes from Paul's less theological letters such as 1 & 2 Corinthians. But neither of us would deny that what the other is reading is inspired. This is a sort of "practical" canon within a canon.

But I agree with the statement here to the extent that someone who defines a separate canon while denying the inspiration of other writings separates himself from the community, because the concept of a canon is an expression of the community. When the "canon within a canon" becomes more than a practical choice for my own spiritual walk and one starts denigrating the authority of other scriptures for other people, then there is a cause for concern.

But setting the words of Jesus against the words of Paul is another matter. First, there is the simple point that God chose to give the scriptures through different writers at different times and in different places. There is evidence of these differences in the writings. I believe a greater danger is the homogenizing of these differences that God put into scripture. It is not honoring scripture, or the God of scripture, to pretend that it is not constructed the way it is.

When you homogenize scripture, on the grounds that it all comes from God, you immediately lose the nuances.

But more importantly, this phrase is a code-word for those who build a theology out of Paul's writings and use it as a basis to ignore the words of Jesus. Jesus talks about holiness of life and obeying the law; Paul speaks against the law. It is essential to their theology to keep people from setting the words of Jesus against **their interpretation** of Paul. It is common in discussion or in theological writings for them to use the words of Jesus and Paul equally because both, they say, are inspired.

But to truly honor scripture, one must note that Paul's words were written to a different audience than were those of Jesus. If one takes the differences seriously, then one will have to deal with what Jesus says brings salvation, and what Paul says brings salvation. One will need to deal with issues of behavior and holiness. When you homogenize scripture, on the grounds that it all comes from God, you immediately lose these nuances, and will form a theology that may be more systematic, but is less faithful to the experience of God reflected in scripture.

In addition, those who form theology from Paul in this way tend to form their theology largely from the more theological books of

Romans and Galatians, and particularly from the parts where Paul expresses his theological foundation. But salvation is also discussed in 1 Corinthians, with much less theology and much more practical application, and in both Romans and Galatians, when Paul gets down to application, he sounds much more like Jesus. One possibility that must be examined here is that modern readers have misunderstood Paul's basic theology and its application, and may need to check their application against Paul's.

For example, the conclusion of some that one can be saved without the fruit of faith is clearly challenged starting with Galatians 5. Theologians have found many ways to work around this, but all of these ignore some aspect of the text.

Let me quote just one passage from Paul, though I will note that Paul regularly gets into discussion of the proper behavior, and does so after he has discussed the nature of the salvation provided by grace. I will take my example from Galatians, known as Paul's strongest statement of salvation, though some might suggest Romans was even stronger. (I wouldn't bother to argue with either!)

> *Those who belong to Christ Jesus have crucified the flesh with its passions and desires.*

> [16]*Live by the Spirit, I say, and do not gratify the desires of the flesh. [17]For what the flesh desires is opposed to the Spirit, and what the Spirit desires is opposed to the flesh; for these are opposed to each other, to prevent you from doing what you want. [18]But if you are led by the Spirit, you are not subject to the law.*

> [19]*Now the works of the flesh are obvious: fornication, impurity, licentiousness, [20]idolatry, sorcery, enmities, strife, jealousy, anger, quarrels, dissensions, factions, [21]envy, drunkenness, carousing, and things like these. I*

am warning you, as I warned you before: **those who do such things will** *not* **inherit the kingdom of God.** *[22]By contrast, the fruit of the Spirit is love, joy, peace, patience, kindness, generosity, faithfulness, [23]gentleness, and self-control. There is no law against such things. [24]And those who belong to Christ Jesus have crucified the flesh with its passions and desires. [25]If we live by the Spirit, let us also be guided by the Spirit* — Galatians 5:16-25 NRSV, emphasis mine.

Here Paul, who has proclaimed grace received by faith nonetheless says that those who practice the evil things he lists will not inherit the kingdom of God. I would suggest again, that while Paul would strongly state that salvation is always by faith, he would expect that faith to be one that produced fruit, just as all of the other Biblical writers or sources we have quoted thus far. He continues by contrasting the fleshly life with what the life of the spirit actually is.

Don't limit what one Bible writer can say based on principles gleaned from another.

Thus while I have some agreement on the point of a canon within a canon, I must reject what I believe is the real thrust of this statement. One cannot simply combine texts from Jesus, Paul, and other writers on the basis that all come from God. One must understand the overall view of each one and then see how they mesh. One must not limit what Jesus can say based on what he **must** be saying because of some theological principle gleaned from Paul.

Let me also repeat one last time: If you are a Christian who believes the incarnation, you must logically believe that Jesus is more important than any other person, whether a writer of scripture or not. Jesus is central.

GLOSSARY

Bible - in this paper used to refer to the books of the canon accepted by protestants. I believe that many books in the apocrypha are inspired, but I wished to limit the extent of the discussion.

Calvinism – named for John Calvin, a theological system whose most noted feature is the doctrine of the sovereignty of God, most commonly seen in the doctrine of predestination.

Canonization - concerning scripture, the acceptance of a book as authoritative by a church or community.

Form Criticism – the study of orally transmitted portions of a written text.

Genre Criticism – the study of the genre or category of documents, such as whole books of the Bible.

Hebrew Scriptures - also known to Christians as the Old Testament.

Historical-Critical method - an approach which views the text using a set of critical methodologies in its historical context, and from a naturalistic perspective. The text is assumed to have meaning and relevance to its immediate audience.

LXX – or Septuagint, Greek translation started in the 3rd century BCE which provides an early witness to a form of the Hebrew text that is now only available in fragments.

Maj - Majority text of the Greek New Testament. A text built strictly by counting the total number of manuscripts, regardless of date, which support each reading, then accepting that reading supported by the greatest number of manuscripts.

MT - Masoretic text, a text of the Hebrew scriptures preserved by the group of scholars known as Masoretes in the 6th through 9th centuries CE. This is essentially the Hebrew text found in modern Hebrew Bibles.

NASB – New American Standard Bible, very literal modern English version, favored by conservative and evangelical Christians.

NIV – New International Version, a modern English Bible version that has characteristics of both dynamic and functional equivalence translation in about equal measure. It is very popular amongst evangelical Christians.

NRSV – New Revised Standard Version, modern English version often regarded as liberal. It is primarily a formal equivalence version in the tradition of the King James Version.

Original sin – the doctrine that all human beings inherit the guilt for Adam's sin, generally coupled with some form of the doctrine of total depravity which states that human beings in their natural state cannot even seek to do anything good.

Pelagianism – named for Pelagius, a monk and opponent of Augustine. Pelagius maintained that human beings were born with the ability to choose either good or evil.

Pentateuch - the first five books of the Bible, Genesis, Exodus, Leviticus, Numbers and Deuteronomy. Also in the narrow sense equivalent to the written Torah.

Predestination – the doctrine that God has chosen certain persons to be saved and others to be lost, and that this choice is made by his sovereignty without regard to any merit or choice on their part.

Prevenient grace – grace given by God prior to any asking or seeking on the part of human beings. This grace makes it possible for one to seek God.

REB – Revised English Bible, modern English Bible version translated in England. It uses the dynamic equivalence approach to translation and has a formal and dignified literary style.

Redaction Criticism – the study of how ancient documents were edited in order to produce a final form.

Rhetorical Criticism – the study of how a text is structured to persuade an audience.

Scientific Bible Study - studying the historical meaning of a passage in context using the best historical methods available. This is how one determines what the passage originally meant to the speaker and to the hearer at the time it was first spoken. It does not refer to relating accomplishments in the natural sciences to Biblical statements.

Septuagint – or LXX, Greek translation started in the 3rd century BCE which provides an early witness to a form of the Hebrew text that is now only available in fragments.

Tanak (sometimes Tanakh) - the Hebrew scriptures. I use this term rather than Old Testament both out of respect for the Jewish canon, and because I find the division into Old and New Testaments inappropriate.

Textual criticism – the process of determining the most likely original text from a set of manuscripts that differ in various ways.

Torah - broadly the first five books of the Bible and the associated oral Torah and teaching surrounding this.

TR - Textus Receptus, or received text. The text which developed from the work of Erasmus and others which in most cases agrees with the majority of Greek manuscripts, but in some texts, such as 1 John 5:7,8 accepts readings which are practically unknown except in very late manuscripts.

Verbal Dictation – the belief that each word of the Bible was dictated by God and the Bible writers were merely God's pens.

Verbal Plenary Inspiration – the belief that each and every word of the Bible is chosen and protected by God. Prophets can be permitted to choose their own words, but each and every word is important and must be protected.

Wesleyan-Arminianism – in soteriology the view that people are not predestined to heaven or hell but are given a choice, made possible by prevenient grace.

TOPICAL INDEX

Scripture Index

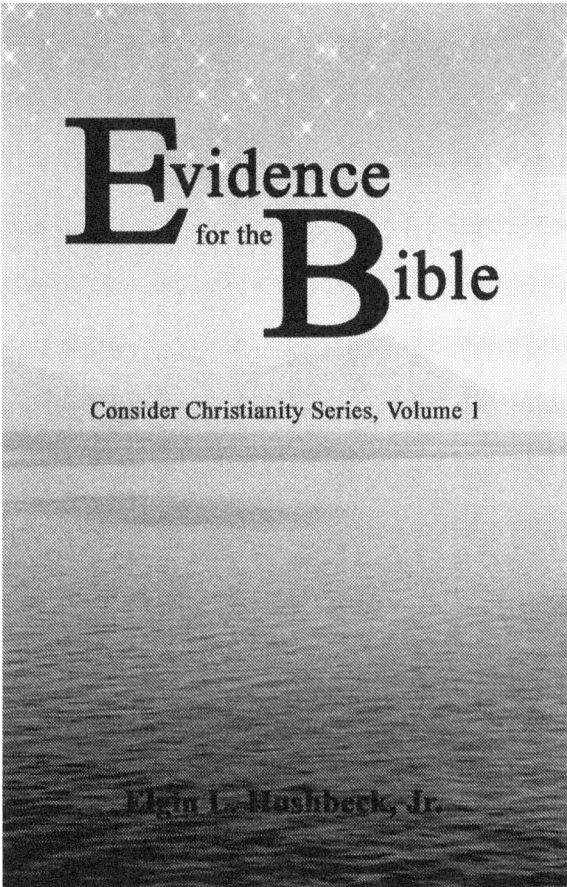

In *Evidence for the Bible*, engineer and former atheist Elgin Hushbeck, Jr. discusses the evidence for the reliability of the Bible clearly and with conviction. Every member of the church who needs to answer questions about faith will benefit from reading this book. You'll want to keep it on your self as a reference.

Price: $16.99
Order from Energion Publications, or from your local or online bookstore.
Web: http://www.energionpubs.com
Phone: (850) 968-1001

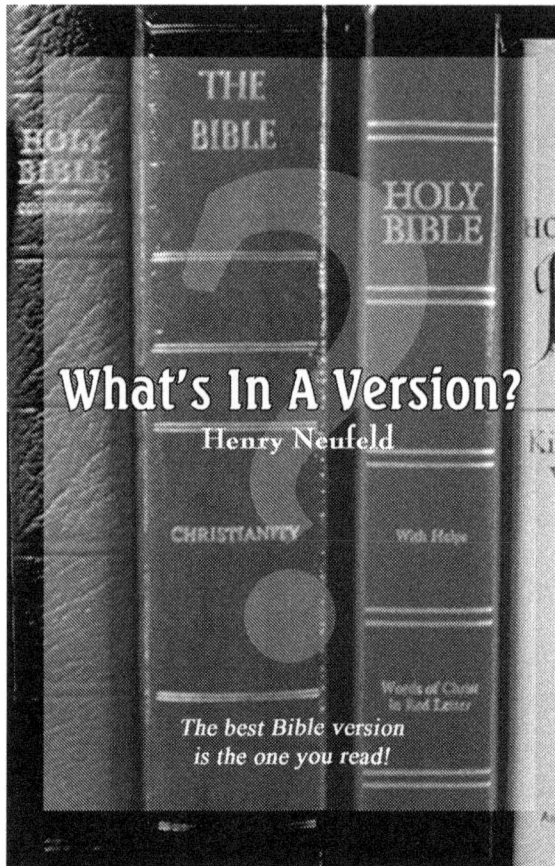

What's In A Version?
Henry Neufeld

*The best Bible version
is the one you read!*

Henry E. Neufeld writes about Bible translations from his knowledge as a student of Biblical languages, and his experience teaching them to laypeople and discussing them on the internet. Many people have questions about translations because they do not understand how translations are produced. Much of the material available is either polarizing, or is provided to advocate a particular version. *What's in a Version?* strives to provide a basis for lay students to understand how translations are made so they can understand the arguments and become confident of the Bible version they choose to use for reading and study.

Price: $12.99
Order from Energion Publications, or from your local or online bookstore.
Web: http://www.energionpubs.com
Phone: (850) 968-1001

NOT ASHAMED OF THE GOSPEL

Confessions of a Liberal Charismatic

HENRY E. NEUFELD

If love is the royal law, why are so many Christians unloving? What is it that makes us put doctrinal issues ahead of people? Henry Neufeld discusses Christianity in the modern world, combining a firm belief in a God who is still with us with a concern for living rich, constructive lives.

Price: $12.99
Order from Energion Publications, or from your local or online bookstore.
Web: http://www.energionpubs.com
Phone: (850) 968-1001

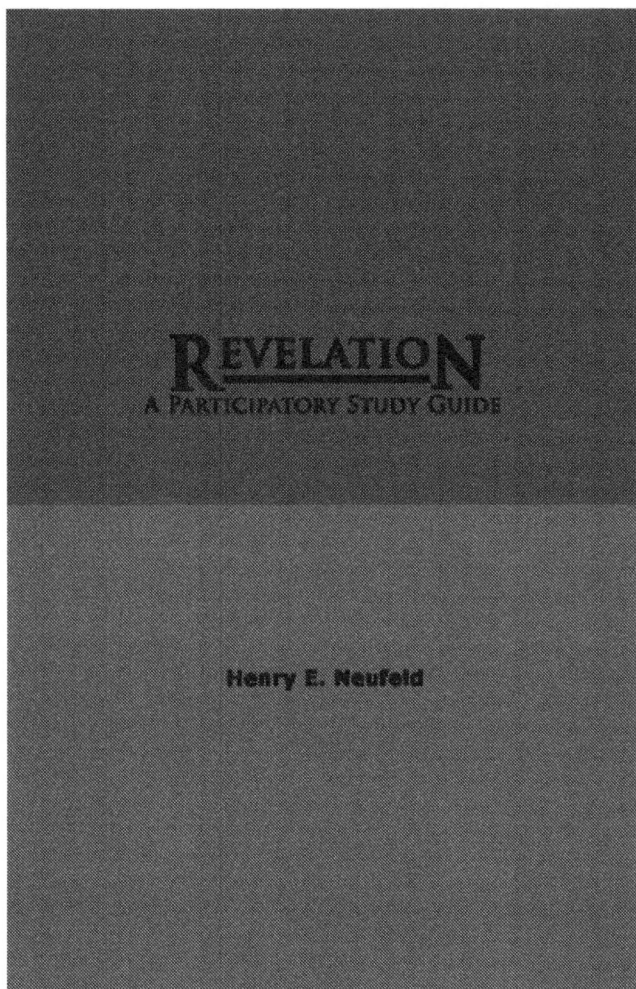

REVELATION
A PARTICIPATORY STUDY GUIDE

Henry E. Neufeld

How do you apply these principles of inspiration in practice? This study guide will help you work your way through the often obscure book of Revelation looking for spiritual truths that are immediately applicable to your life.

Price: $9.99
Order from Energion Publications, or from your local or online bookstore.
Web: http://www.energionpubs.com
Phone: (850) 968-1001

www.ingramcontent.com/pod-product-compliance
Lightning Source LLC
Chambersburg PA
CBHW022118080426
42734CB00006B/174